W9-CAD-074

# THE THUNDER

# OF SILENCE

BY JOEL S. GOLDSMITH

*The Altitude of Prayer*
*The Art of Meditation*
*The Art of Spiritual Healing*
*Awakening Mystical Consciousness*
*Consciousness Is What I Am*
*The Gift of Love*
*Living Between Two Worlds*
*Living the Infinite Way*
*The Mystical I*
*Our Spiritual Resources*
*A Parenthesis in Eternity*
*Practicing the Presence*
*The Thunder of Silence*
*The World Is New*

# THE THUNDER OF SILENCE

EDITED BY
LORRAINE SINKLER

**HARPER & ROW, PUBLISHERS**, **New York**
Cambridge, Hagerstown, Philadelphia, San Francisco,
London, Mexico City, São Paulo, Sydney

> Except the Lord build the house, they
> labour in vain that build it.
> —Psalm 127

Illumination dissolves all material ties and binds men together with the golden chains of spiritual understanding; it acknowledges only the leadership of the Christ; it has no ritual or rule but the divine, impersonal, universal Love, no other worship than the inner Flame that is ever lit at the shrine of Spirit. This union is the free state of spiritual brotherhood. The only restraint is the discipline of Soul; therefore, we know liberty without license; we are a united universe without physical limits, a divine service to God without ceremony or creed. The illumined walk without fear—by Grace.

—THE INFINITE WAY

# CONTENTS

7

## PART THREE

### FROM LAW TO GRACE

# INTRODUCTION

Revelation always comes as somewhat of a shock, not only to the person who receives the revelation, but also to those with whom it is shared. It is the nature of revelation to be shocking and startling because when it hits up against our cherished beliefs, we become conscious of the degree to which our minds have been conditioned by the opinions and theories current in human thinking, and suddenly realize the extent of our unenlightenment.

It is not long ago that the majority of people lived a wholly materialistic life, believing that the only real things of life were the material ones and the only real power a physical power. Into that world was introduced the idea that there is a world of mind and mind-power, and this so permeated consciousness that the focus of attention was shifted from the material to the mental.

Had it not been for revelation, I, too, would have lived out my life in this world of mind, never realizing that the world of mind-power is as illusory as that of material power; but one day a message came to me that mind is not power, that thought is not power. This shocked me, steeped as I had been in the teaching that "right thinking" could solve all my problems.

There were many unfoldments following that one, and now after several years of becoming accustomed to these startling revelations and of giving the message time to permeate consciousness, it is being given to the public in this book where you will read something which may sound so familiar to you that your immediate response may be, "Everybody knows this"; but I can assure you that if people did, they would all be dedicated Souls on the spiritual path. Insofar as I have observed from my study of the spiritual literature of the world, the truth stated in this book has never been fully revealed although it constitutes the absolute basis for true spiritual living.

Before you read any further, let me assure you that I have no interest whatsoever in establishing a new religion or a new religious teaching, or in setting up any person or group of persons to be obeyed whose dictates and opinions are in any way considered binding, final, or infallible. I have no intention or desire to leave behind me any kind of religious organization—anything that anyone can join, promote, publicize, or use for personal profit, or even anything that anyone can feel he can rely upon for his salvation. If there is anything that I would like most of all to do in my span of life on earth, it is to remove from man all those props or crutches upon which he has relied.

The purpose of this book is not to put you in bondage to any person or organization. Rather is its purpose to set you free from "man, whose breath is in his nostrils," free to unite with all those who are on the same spiritual path, free to share with those who are seeking the spiritual way, but in bondage to nobody, belonging to nobody, owing "no man anything, but to love one another." That is the real freedom, and nothing less than that freedom can house God. Do not believe for a moment that God can be in anything, not even in The Infinite Way. God cannot be in anything, and the only way that you can know God is to be free—mentally and spiritually free.

"Where the Spirit of the Lord is, there is liberty"—that is where liberty is; that is where real freedom is, where strength is. The only strength there is, is in union with God, and that is an infinity of strength. Union of the human variety changes with the changing and unstable world. If we have learned nothing else through these centuries of wars, we have learned how fleeting is power. In all the covenants that have been made—all the treaties and other international agreements— there has been no lasting strength.

The only real strength there is, is in conscious union with God and in a realization of the true nature of spiritual power. When we have that realization, one with God becomes a majority. One individual having the spiritual understanding of the nature of God becomes a law of harmony, health, and supply unto thousands and thousands of people all over the world. That is where the strength is—in union with God.

For centuries, country after country has been seeking its freedom. Many a country has temporarily found what it thought was freedom only to find itself enslaved later on by something more powerful than that from which it had broken free.

It is not possible to get free *from* anything. This is a hard saying, bitter in the mouth and even more bitter in the belly. There are thousands of people trying to free themselves from husbands or wives, thinking that when that particular freedom is gained their lot is going to be a better one. Sometimes it is, temporarily; but even if it is, it is only a human solution, not permanent and real, because no one ever gets free *from*. To become free from one thing is to become attached to another thing. There is no freedom *from* anything: The only complete freedom is a freedom *in* Christ.

To leave one religious organization to join another is to find freedom from one only to become involved in another. That is not freedom. Nor can a person find spiritual freedom by leaving one country for another, even though he may im-

prove his material lot as has been demonstrated by the millions of immigrants to the North American continent who
have improved their physical well-being. The mere change
of locale, however, does not necessarily mean peace, happiness, safety, or security because not one of these can be found
in flags, countries, or continents—they cannot even be found
in health or wealth, but only in the realization of God, which
brings a release from fear of what man can do, or from circumstances or conditions.

Harmony is found, not by exchanging one condition of
bondage for another, but by coming out from under the law
and living under that Grace which is the gift of God. For
a while, unfortunately, there remain the thousand on our
left and the ten thousand on our right who will not accept
the grace of God and who brought forth from the Master
his sorrowful, "O Jerusalem, Jerusalem . . . how often would
I have gathered thy children together, even as a hen gather-
eth her chickens under her wings, and ye would not!" This
is the one remaining sorrow after we have attained our own
freedom, this sorrow of looking at our parents, children, sisters, or brothers, our husband or wife, our fellow countrymen,
and thinking, "Why can't you accept this thing that I have
found?" But the longer we are on this path the easier it will
be for us to understand that it is not possible for anyone to
embrace truth except in proportion to his readiness for it.

Sometimes that readiness comes only because of the futility
and frustration that have gone before. Every sin, every disease, and every lack that have ever touched our lives have
been a necessary part of our entire experience without which
we would not have been made ready or prepared to receive
the unfoldment of a truly spiritual message. I say this knowing that some of us have been down into the very depths
where sin, disease, and lack are greatest, while others have
had very little with which to contend. Yet whatever the degree of the severity of the problem each one has had, it is
perhaps the degree that each one has needed. Some cannot
go up to the heights of spiritual vision until they have gone

all the way down physically, mentally, morally, or financially. Some have had to go only halfway down, and some probably much less than that; but whatever depths you and I have known, that was the experience necessary for us to reach the heights.

Some of you may yet have to be pushed and prodded very hard and involved in a great many serious problems before you will be able to embrace the principles set forth in this book; whereas some of you will absorb them very easily and without having any harassing problems to overcome. That, too, depends upon what degree of unfoldment you bring to this work.

This message is proved true only as it is individually demonstrated, and because of that it should be easy to understand why attempting to organize a religion around such a teaching or asking people to join anything as intangible as this would in no way contribute to the objective of The Infinite Way, which is that these principles permeate human consciousness and become tangible in individual experience. If any attempt were made to organize this teaching, it would be of benefit to no one; if monthly or annual dues were paid, it would be to no purpose; if mighty temples were built to enshrine these principles, or statues erected of the man who taught them, it would be of no avail.

One thing alone will demonstrate this teaching—realizing what the principles are and then taking them into your heart and mind and soul and body, living with them, moving and having your being in them, with them, and through them, until they become demonstrable principles within you. Then you become the light of the world, a world which may be bounded only by your immediate family or community, or which may be one so vast in its scope that it includes the entire globe. No two will be led in the same way; no two will evolve in the same manner. It all depends upon the degree of your individual unfoldment.

The entire message of this book is based on the principle that there is an inner Grace which does not operate through, or by, physical might or mental powers. This Grace, of which most people are unaware, operates only when faith in anything and everything has been relinquished, even including faith in a God from whom the world has been expecting miracles and for whom the world has been waiting since the beginning of time.

There have been many in the history of the world who have known this secret, and each of these of whom we have knowledge has imparted it to a group of people who became his disciples or followers. In every instance, however, after one or two generations, the teaching was adulterated, and its heart and soul disappeared from the face of the earth, only to be revealed to someone again in a later age, after which the same process was repeated.

In the face of this, it is natural to ask whether it is worthwhile to attempt to teach it again. Is it worthwhile to travel thousands of miles year in and year out to carry such a message to the world, if only a few people receive and demonstrate it, and then let it pass from the earth again? And my answer to that is that the circumstances are different today.

In all past generations, the world could look forward to the discovery of an increasingly greater power, and in each generation some greater power was discovered, but today with atomic power an actuality the world is faced with the ultimate of power. Who can vision anything beyond nuclear power? Is there anything beyond this, or has the world now reached the end of its search for power?

The truth in *The Thunder of Silence* can be found in the New Testament. Readers of this book, however, cannot expect that the mere reading of it will enable them to live by its revealed principles. Those who feel no response to the unfoldment presented here will, of course, be more than satisfied with one reading, but those who feel a thrill of recognition in their first reading should make this book their constant companion day and night, Sundays and holidays, until their materialistic state of consciousness begins to yield and surrenders itself as the transcendental Consciousness takes over the mind, body, and everyday experience of their lives.

More than thirty years of experience have demonstrated beyond doubt that this change of consciousness can take place in any person who continues to abide in this message. Such a change of consciousness must take place within the reader before he will find it possible to live by the I-say-unto-you of the Sermon on the Mount.

The purpose of this book is to reveal transcendental Consciousness and thereby develop individual consciousness to that place where one can truthfully say, "I live; yet not I, but Christ liveth in me." This purpose can be achieved only by dwelling—living, moving, and having one's being—and by continuously abiding in the Word.

JOEL S. GOLDSMITH

*Box 5308 Pawaa Station*
*Honolulu, Hawaii*

## PART ONE

# FROM DARKNESS

# TO LIGHT

# CHAPTER I

## THE TWO COVENANTS

For it is written, that Abraham had two sons, the one by a bondmaid, the other by a freewoman.

But he who was of the bondwoman was born after the flesh; but he of the freewoman was by promise.

Which things are an allegory: for these are the two covenants; the one from the mount Sinai, which gendereth to bondage, which is Agar. . . .

But Jerusalem which is above is free, which is the mother of us all.

GALATIANS 4:22–24, 26

In our humanhood, we are sons of the bondwoman, in subjection to the flesh and its claims, in bondage to the things, thoughts, and activities of the flesh, whether it be this flesh of the body or the flesh called money or other forms of human living. Living in and through the flesh as the offspring of the bondwoman, we are under the laws of matter, the laws of economics, and the laws of race, religion, and nationality —under the covenant "which gendereth to bondage." The other covenant is that of our spiritual adoption, which comes through a conscious activity within our own consciousness and at a time when we are prepared for that transition, because the transition from humanhood to spiritual sonship is made only by Grace.

When a person says that he would like to be a child of God and be free of the burdens of the flesh, usually he does not really mean it. What he means is that he would like to be free of the burdens of the flesh, but retain the pleasures and the profits of the flesh. It is for this reason that as human beings we cannot choose to be children of God.

But there does come a time in the consciousness of every one of us—with some now and with some many lifetimes from now—when, through an inner Grace, we are able and willing not only to be rid of the ills of the flesh, but also of the pleasures and profits of the flesh, and to become acquainted with our spiritual identity or Selfhood, with that new creature—not the old one made healthy, not the old one made honorable, but a new creature which is born of the Spirit. This is the transitional experience.

To be born of the Spirit means to be reborn through a transition of consciousness, and this rebirthing can occur while we are on this very plane of consciousness known as the earth, or it can take place after we have left this sphere. It is well to remember that if we fail to make the transition here, there will always be the opportunity for us to make it hereafter because in the kingdom of God there is no time. There it is always now, and this now is always presenting itself to us with fresh opportunities.

This moment is now. This moment—this now—we have the opportunity to reject our humanness and accept the divinity of our being. But if it is beyond our immediate capacity to do that at this moment, later on tonight we shall discover that it is also now, and in that nowness, we are again face to face with the opportunity to accept or reject the divinity of our being. If we are not prepared to receive it then, there will be tomorrow afternoon, next year, or the year after; and each time that the opportunity to realize our divine sonship comes to our thought, it will be now. A hundred years from now, it will be now to us.

Now is always the time to accept our divinity, but while that now may come to us at this moment, to some it may have come years ago and to some it may come years hence. Whether or not it comes at this particular hour of the clock or some other hour, whenever it comes, it will be now. Each of us has to face every moment of every day unto eternity, and those of us who, for one reason or another, are not able at this particular time to accept the covenant of our liberty, the liberty wherewith we are "clothed upon" when we accept Christhood, will still have a new and fresh opportunity throughout all ages.

Those who have gone on before us as human beings and have left our visible sight, some in gross spiritual darkness and some in actual sin and degradation, also exist now, and they, too, have the same opportunity now that they had when they rejected it here on earth, only now they may have developed a greater capacity to accept it.

What does it mean to accept the spiritual dispensation in our experience? Unless we understand what it is that constitutes this spiritual dispensation, we cannot be prepared to accept it.

Regardless of the fact that the majority of people pay lip service to a belief in God, many of them do not believe in God. True, they may believe that there is a God or have a belief about God, but they have no faith, no realization, no conviction, because the nature of the bondman is to be in bondage to effect—to love, worship, and fear anything that has form, that is visible as effect. It may be bodily health—the heart, liver, or lungs—or it may be dollar bills, investments, or home, but the love and devotion and fear of most human beings are always directed at someone or something in the visible realm.

The son of the bondwoman is in bondage as long as some thought, thing, or person is necessary, and that is what constitutes humanhood. The new covenant of the new creature begins in the moment when we realize, " 'I and my Father are one,' and all that the Father has is mine. I look in no other direction than to the Infinite Invisible. Then what appears from within, I share gloriously, freely, joyously."

The transition into divine sonship brings about that change from faith in the visible to faith in the Infinite Invisible, in that which can never be seen, heard, tasted, touched, smelled —or even thought or reasoned. There has to be a faith without a reason for that faith. There must be an all-consuming inner conviction which agrees with this faith, even while not knowing what it is—an inner instinct, an inner intuition, an inner grace.

"There shall no sign be given": The signs *follow* them that believe. When the faith comes, the signs follow. If we are given any sign, any thing, or any thought to which we can cling, then that thing or that thought is that upon which our faith rests instead of upon the Invisible which is God.

It is possible to think and think on truth—and up to a certain point that is normal, natural, and right—but then there must come a time when thought stops, a blank comes, almost a vacuum, and then into that vacuum rush the very presence and power of God. We can only come into that Presence stark naked, in a moment of complete silence, when the entire thought processes have stopped, when we have nothing upon which to rely, nothing on which to pin our hopes, but when we have made ourselves barren and completely empty.

That is the moment when we perceive that, even when we cannot know It or feel It or think It, there is an invisible Presence, an intangible Something, which nevertheless is operating, and then from that very Invisibility will come into expression everything necessary to our unfoldment. If we think ourselves to be something, we gravely err. It is only when we come to that place of self-renunciation that the divine Selfhood of our own being reveals Itself. Silence is the way.

The Silence is not an absence of sound, but is a state of consciousness which enables us to refrain from mental reaction to what is seen or heard. For example, we may see and recognize a shadow on the wall—an ugly appearance—and yet have no reaction of fear, knowing it to be a shadow.

When consciousness has attained the awareness of one power, one law, one substance, one cause—oneness—we do not respond with fear, doubt, or horror to anything seen or heard, and then it is that consciousness has gone beyond power and attained the Silence—the healing consciousness.

# CHAPTER II

# KARMIC LAW

All the suffering the world is experiencing today is because of a sense of separation from God, because it has not accepted a God who is "closer . . . than breathing, nearer than hands and feet," a God who is not only able but willing and desirous that we bear fruit richly.

In paganistic times, probably out of a sense of gratitude, people worshiped whatever it was that seemed to bless them, and began to endow those things with the powers of Deity. As men rose higher in consciousness, there appeared the teaching of one God, but apparently men were not prepared for a realization of God as God really is, and so we find a very strange kind of a God in Hebrew Scripture.

Just as we know that the sun, moon, and stars are not God, so do we know now that the Jehovah God of wrath and vengeance is not God. The God of the Old Testament is not God: It is karmic law. It is the law that says that *as ye sow, so shall ye reap.* It is the law that says that if we do good, good will come to us, but, on the other hand, if we do evil, evil will come upon us.

As a man "thinketh in his heart, so is he." That is not God: That is karmic law which came to be known as God. It never was God, as John realized when he revealed that "the law was given by Moses, but grace and truth came by Jesus Christ." There is a great difference between the grace and truth of Christ Jesus and the law of Moses. There is a world of difference between karmic law and God, and while it is necessary for everyone to know and understand karmic law, it is also vitally necessary that one go beyond this age-old law into the realm of Grace. We shall never accomplish this by violating karmic law, but only by understanding its meaning and place in our life.

The Ten Commandments, with which we are all familiar, constitute part of that law: For example, there is the command, "Honour thy father and thy mother." Would anyone call that a very spiritual teaching? Anyone who has been touched by the Spirit of God, even in the slightest degree, would be unable to do other than to honor his father and mother and to love his neighbor as himself.

Is there anyone who would even dream of having the presumption to tell Christ Jesus, John of Patmos, Buddha, or Lao-tse to honor his mother and father or to love his neighbor as himself? Would anyone who has been touched by the Spirit of God have to be told not to be bigoted, biased, or prejudiced against races and religions?

Such laws are for human beings who have not even reached the state of being very high human beings, but are in such a low state of consciousness that they still need to be reminded that they must not envy their neighbor's property, his wife, or his farm. True, there is a time in our lives during our earliest stages of humanhood when we need the law, when we need to be told how to act toward one another, but if we remain in that state we will not advance very rapidly toward our spiritual freedom.

Everyone on earth must some day inhabit heaven. Everyone on earth must some day rise above being a sick and sinning mortal and accept the inheritance of his divine sonship, but no one will be able to do this by living under the law, nor will he do it by learning to be a good human being. It cannot be accomplished merely by some human form of worship, nor by becoming honest or moral. Those are only first steps.

Only by losing our carnal desires, our mortal, selfish, human desires, do we prove that we are making advances toward a higher state of humanhood. Ultimately, there comes a day when we actually attain a realization of the Spirit of God that dwells in us, when we come face to face with It, when It touches us on the shoulder, on the head, or in the heart, when in some way or other, It announces Its presence. From then on, we are no longer simply good men or women; from then on we are no longer under the law of punishment or of reward: From that time to the end of our days on earth and throughout eternity, we are under Grace.

Then it is that we begin to catch the first glimpse of this great truth that all we have been doing throughout our many struggling days is living under karmic law, violating it or coming into agreement with it, believing that if we are good today, the good things of the world will flow to us, but that we can cheat ourselves of them tomorrow by being bad.

We are told that if we sin, God will punish us, but that was the Old Testament version of God, and no such teaching appears in the New Testament sayings of Jesus Christ. On the contrary, it is made clear that God has more pleasure in one sinner who comes to the realization of God than in ninety-nine people who just walk the earth as good people. Should it not cause us to stop to think that all the ninety-nine good people do not please God as much as the one sinner?

The God of most people on earth is a God that punishes evil and rewards good, and there is no such God. We do not have to fear God and we do not have to attempt to influence God or sacrifice to God. God is the same to the saint and to the sinner. God is good; God is love; God is the eternal, immortal, spiritual, creative principle of the universe,

its maintaining and sustaining principle; but can anyone believe that God is that today and then because we happen to
make a mistake tomorrow God becomes something else?

It is little wonder that the Hebrew world reacted violently
when it heard Jesus Christ preach that God has no pleasure
in animal sacrifices or even in monetary sacrifices. The people
of those days believed that God had to be pleased, God had
to be assuaged and placated; they believed that God could
in some way be influenced by a person's conduct. It is much
the same today when some devout worshipers light a candle
to God, tithe—thinking to bribe God—or observe fast or feast
days, all subconsciously done with the idea that such conduct
can influence God to act favorably in their behalf.

God never rewards virtue. God never punishes sin. True,
sin is punished—by the sin. In other words, the person who
makes the wrong electrical connection will be burned, but he
cannot blame the electricity for this. The electricity did not
punish him: He brought about his own punishment by his
incorrect act. The person who goes into the water, becomes
frightened, flounders around, and finally almost drowns cannot blame the water, but rather, his ignorance of how to be-
have in the water. No one can violate law and not be punished for such violation; but no one should blame God for
the ensuing punishment. The fault lies not in God but in
individual conduct and in individual misperception of the
nature of the law.

Once we understand that there is a karmic law and that
human beings are subject to that law, our first task will be
to bring ourselves into harmony with it. In other words, if
there is a punishment for stealing, we must first learn to stop
stealing. If there is a punishment for lying, we must train
ourselves not to lie, even if at the moment some good seems
to be derived from indulging in falsehood. True, we might
lie or cheat in our business and thereby gain some temporary
profit, but if we understand that any lying, deceiving, or
cheating that we do will ultimately wreck us, we shall more
than likely begin to train ourselves not to indulge in un-

scrupulous methods or actions in our personal, social, and business life. The first attempt, then, when we understand that there is a karmic law, is to free ourselves from the evils that will bring evil consequences upon us.

It is undoubtedly better to live in such a state of consciousness than to live in a lower one, but we should nevertheless realize that this stage of life is actually the Hebraic stage as lived under the *thou shalt nots* of Moses: Thou shalt not do this, and then thou wilt not bring upon thy head a punishment. Thou shalt not covet thy neighbor's house, and then thou wilt not bring trouble upon thyself. Thou shalt not steal; thou shalt not commit murder; thou shalt honor thy father and thy mother, which means that thou shalt not forget them or ignore them or treat them unkindly. There is no arguing the fact that when we become obedient to the Ten Commandments, we bring ourselves into harmony with karmic law and benefit by it, but we must not forget that we are still under the law, because another violation tomorrow can bring trouble, and as long as we live only by the Ten Commandments, we are still living humanly and by human laws.

This is the God the greater part of the Bible reveals, but this is not God: This is the law, the Lord God, the Law-God, the karmic law, the law of cause and effect: *As ye sow, so shall ye reap.* That is not God, that is ye—as ye sow, so shall ye reap. It does not mention a thing about God: It just warns us that when we do the right or the wrong kind of sowing, we do the right or the wrong kind of reaping, but surely it must be clear that God has nothing to do with either the sowing or the reaping.

None of this has any real reference to God. It has reference to karmic law, the law of cause and effect, the law as found throughout the Bible. But because this was once believed to be God, it has been perpetuated by people who dare not read the Bible objectively, and so today even though they call themselves Protestants or Catholics, they all go on accepting the same old Hebraic God of the Ten Commandments, the God of cause and effect, the God of karma.

Now let us find out, if we can, what God really is, because on this point our whole experience hinges. It is right and proper to be a good Hebrew, that is, to obey the Ten Commandments. It is right and proper to be an honest businessman instead of a dishonest one, and a healthy human being instead of an unhealthy one. But that has no relationship to the spiritual path, nor to our ultimate destiny, which is to return to the Father's house, to God-consciousness.

In order to achieve our ultimate goal, the nature of God must be understood; and therefore, there must be but one question in our thought and that is: What is God?

First and foremost, we must realize that our prayers and meditations do not influence God—to do good for us or to do evil to us—that we cannot bring the glory of God to ourselves or to anyone else. All that we can do is to recognize that God in the midst of us is mighty, not because of us—it is just that we have been given the grace to recognize the *IS*, that which already *IS*. That is why the Master told the disciples not to glory because the devil was subject unto them, but because their names were written in heaven. That is why no one ever dares take glory unto himself because of a healing, for no human being has ever brought about a healing—it was brought about by a divine state of spiritual being, which operates and can operate only through and as the consciousness of one who knows the nature of God and can therefore bring healing into visible manifestation. That is our part in this glorious spiritual work. That is our only part—to know God, to know God whom to know aright is life eternal.

When we know the nature of God as love and as life eternal, never again will we deal with death, old age, or disease as if it were a reality that we could change by bringing God to it. We shall understand that this has nothing to do with God: It has to do with *as ye sow, so shall ye reap*. If we believe in a law of sin, a law of matter or disease, or a law of punishment, that is the experience that we are bringing into our lives and the lives of those who look to us for spiritual guidance.

When we understand the nature of God as Love, we shall understand the word Grace. Then we shall understand that our good comes by Grace, not by deserving it or being worthy of it. What human being can ever be good enough to deserve God! As a matter of fact, the more of human qualities we have, the more have to be wiped out before we can realize God. We cannot be brought to a place of deserving God— we can only be brought to a place where that part of us which wants to be worthy or appears to be unworthy is thrown out of the way and our true Selfhood is revealed. Our good—physical, mental, moral, and financial—is ours by divine Grace as the gift of God. We cannot earn it or deserve it; we cannot influence God to give it to us, and no act or deed or thought of ours is powerful enough to prevent God from operating and continuing to operate.

Though our sins be scarlet, we are white as snow in the very minute we realize our true identity. True, while we are accepting karma, that is, while we are accepting ourselves as human beings, there may be a law of karma operating in our experience, but that law stops operating as soon as we realize, "I am coming out and becoming separate, and now I am going to live under Grace." The moment we realize that we are living under Grace, we drop the word "I." We stop boasting that "I" is good and worthy and we stop condemning "I" as bad or unworthy.

We even forget the past and come to acknowledge that we did not live an hour ago and that we cannot live an hour hence. The only time we can live is now, and now we are living under Grace. The past is gone; the future will never be: Now we are under Grace. Now there is no sin, no disease, no death, no iniquity—nothing operating in our consciousness except love, the love of God, not your love or mine.

If only we really and truly could come into some measure

of realization of the nature of God, how we would throw the years off our shoulders, how we would throw off the memories of our past acts of omission and commission, how we would throw off the memories of our wrong thinking and begin to understand that now are we the sons of God. Now in this instant of divine Grace, the entire memory of all our past years is gone. Now we are willing to forget our good deeds as well as our bad ones. We are willing to forget the masquerade, the part we have been playing in this particular production, and drop it along with our costume and all that belongs to it.

If we could call to mind the highest and best example of fatherhood we know, we would then see that no real father ever permits animosity, impatience, or intolerance to interfere with his father-love for his son. In such understanding all this nonsense about a punishing God, a God of vengeance, would disappear.

God is too pure to behold iniquity. The Master claimed that he came to earth not to do his own will but the will of the Father. And what is this will of the Father? It is to heal the sick, raise the dead, forgive the sinner. Then, is there a God of punishment? The Master said, "Neither do I condemn thee." Is there a God of punishment? He said to the thief on the cross, "Today shalt thou be with me in paradise." Is there a God of punishment? And he said, "Thy sins be forgiven thee."

There is no record in the entire revelation of the Master of damnation or punishment by him, but there is this: "Sin no more, lest a worse thing come unto thee." Does he say that God will visit it upon us? No, our sin will visit it upon us, not God. The very misdeed will return unto us. We do not even have to perform a sinful deed; we merely have to have a desire for it, a wish for it, as Jesus pointed out when he cautioned against even looking upon a woman with an adulterous thought. One need not carry out the act because the very mental state brings back to one something of its own nature. This is not living under the law of God: This is living under karmic law, because when we are under God there is no possibility of there being any sin.

Current paganistic beliefs that God is going out before us to punish our enemies were brought over from ancient days. So today all over this world people are praying for peace on earth, and they are praying to God for that peace, but God is ignoring them. All over this earth men and women are praying for their children—for their health and their safety— but God is ignoring such requests, too. If God does not answer our prayers for good, what chance is there that God will pay attention to any prayer for evil? What kind of a God do we worship? Has there ever been a race of people on earth so much better than any other race that God would destroy one for the sake of another, or one nation for the sake of another? Have we ever had a perfect race even humanly, or a perfect nation?

During the last century, there have been three major wars, and those who were vanquished were as Christian and democratic as those who were victorious. What a stretch of the imagination it would require to believe, for example, that Russia was on the winning side of the war because it was Christian and democratic! Is it not clear that God has been given credit and God has been damned for things for which God had no responsibility?

As long as we accept the law of an eye for an eye and a tooth for a tooth, we are setting in operation the karmic law. As we do unto another, that is what is done unto us. In our criminal courts, this ancient law is carried out by sentencing to death a man who has committed murder; yet, on the other hand, when a government sends the men and women of its nation out to commit murder on a mass scale, it dares to hope that they will not be murdered in return. But that is because it knows nothing about karmic law and the inevitability of karmic law. There is no escaping the penalty for the violation of the Ten Commandments. There is a punishment for every violation, but it is not a punishment from God: It is a punishment that comes to us as a result of the act or thought that we have set in motion.

In other words, we are creating our tomorrows by our to-days. Everything that we do today determines something that is going to happen in our life tomorrow or tomorrow's tomorrow. Very often we wonder why certain disasters come into our experience, thinking that we do not deserve them—but that is not true. We do deserve them, if not personally, then because of our being a part of the race or national consciousness. As citizens of a country, we are responsible for the acts of our government, and when we sanction acts that violate the Ten Commandments, we have set in motion the karmic law and its inevitable results which return to us. The only way that an individual can escape the karmic law of his government is when within himself he disclaims its acts.

When a citizen sanctions the throwing of a bomb which wipes out whole cities, that citizen has entered into the karmic experience of his government, and the day must come when that person is repaid in like coin. If, however, the citizen not only repudiates the act, but actually can go so far as to say, and mean it, "I would rather be hit by a bomb and have my whole family destroyed than approve of my government's destroying another with it," in that state of consciousness, the individual frees himself from the karmic law invoked by that act.

It is not necessary to fight the government; it is not necessary to get up and preach to the government about its sins: It is only necessary that within ourselves we do not come into agreement with any violation of the Ten Commandments.

When the Master gave us the true spiritual religion, he threw nine of those commandments out the window, dropped them entirely, and substituted for them the First Commandment: "Thou shalt love the Lord thy God with all thy heart, and with all thy soul, and with all thy mind," and added to this first one another ancient commandment, "Thou shalt love thy neighbour as thyself." These are the only two commandments to which Jesus gave any spiritual significance, and they are a guide to us in our humanhood.

To "love the Lord thy God with all thy heart, and with all thy soul, and with all thy mind" would be to bring ourselves into obedience to God and God's laws. To love our neighbor as ourselves completely removes us from karmic law because we would then neither think nor do an injustice, a wrong, or an evil to another any more than we would do it unto ourselves or than we would wish to have it done unto ourselves. To pray to God to harm or injure another is a form of pagan ignorance, and to pray to God for one's own personal gain is but another form of paganistic stupidity.

Therefore, in our relationship with one another we are living completely in the sense that we are one, or as the Master counseled, "Call no man your father upon the earth: for one is your Father, which is in heaven." If we look upon one another as brothers and sisters, there is then no karmic effect being generated within us because our life is a life of love, service, devotion, and sharing.

If our relationship to one another is pure, we want nothing from anyone but the opportunity to work, share, or in some way be an instrument of blessing to our other Self. In return we ask for nothing. The opportunity of sharing, loving, and co-operating is enough because all that the Father has is ours, and the Father has means of bringing our supply to us without our desiring it or asking for it.

Such an awareness of our true identity creates a spiritual bond among all those who are on this path. In such a bond, no one is thinking of taking advantage of anyone else; no one is thinking in terms of self-gain, of self-aggrandizement, or of any form of self except the idea of a sharing of the Self.

Eventually, this will be the universal relationship on earth, and the law of an eye for an eye and a tooth for a tooth, the karmic law of punishment, will not be operative in our experience.

The thoughts to which we give expression as human beings

come back upon us because that is the nature of the karmic law of as ye sow, so shall ye reap, but God is not to blame for that. We have set in motion the karmic law, and that is what is returning to us. All of us by the very nature of having been born have been guilty of offenses of omission or commission and have therefore brought ourselves under the operation of karmic law. Naturally, then, the question arises: Can this karmic law be broken? Can it be ended? And the answer is, Yes.

We can stop the operation of karmic law at any moment in our life when we recognize that we have set this law in motion by our own thoughts and deeds or by the acceptance of racial or religious or national consciousness, and then begin renouncing it. The way to break the karmic law is through repentance and by living constantly in an atmosphere of love and forgiveness. Then we are no longer human or mortal because we no longer harbor thoughts and deeds of mortality.

From then on the only karma that comes into our experience is racial or national, and this, too, we must disavow in our own consciousness. If there were a war tomorrow and if we should be called to service, we must answer that call. We "render . . . unto Caesar the things which are Caesar's"— we must fulfill our obligations as citizens because if we do not do our part, we are only removing ourselves from that temporary trouble by compelling someone else to serve in our place and putting someone else in the position where we should be. This is far worse than ourselves accepting the call to service because at least in answering that call we can disavow the act and pray as earnestly for the enemy as for ourselves. We can pray for the freedom, safety, and security of the enemy and, even while rendering "unto Caesar the things which are Caesar's," thereby free ourselves from the penalty of the karmic law by performing whatever is required of us as citizens without hate or vengeance and with detachment.

Only one thing can free us from the law of as ye sow, so shall ye reap—to stop sowing. The only way to stop sowing is to recognize our spiritual identity because then we need not reach out, scheming, plotting, planning, grasping, or even desiring that which another has, but we can be beholders and watch what wonderful ways the Father has of providing for us without depriving another.

In The Infinite Way we recognize that there is a law, but we also recognize that there is something called Grace. Let me illustrate it in this way. If we have not been taught in modern metaphysics, we are subject to material laws because there are laws of matter to plague us on this human plane—laws of climate, infection, heredity, environment, time, and space. Every human being in the world is under the law of time. In fact, all we have to do is to look at a calendar long enough and we begin to feel weary, weak, and depleted.

Those of you who have had any experience at all with metaphysical or spiritual healing have already learned that these laws of matter are not power in the presence of spiritual understanding. They are theories and beliefs, but there is a Grace which sets them aside. That does not mean that on the human level there is not a law of matter; it does not mean that there is not a law of mind: It merely means that there is a state of Grace that sets aside both the laws of matter and the laws of mind.

When we come under Grace, no laws operate. In the spiritual realm, which is a state of Grace, there are not two powers operating, one over another, one overcoming the other, or one removing the other—there is but one. There is no opposition; there is no contention in the realm of Spirit: There is only a state of Grace which is itself the law of elimination to every phase of materiality. When we come into a state of Grace, we no longer have good health or bad health, nor do we have abundant or meager supply: We live in a state of spirituality in which there is neither good nor evil—no degrees and no comparisons: There is only Being, divine Being, spiritual Being, one Being.

It is only when we stop thinking in terms of health and sickness, wealth and poverty, and begin to think in terms of spirituality that we transcend not only bad humanhood but even good humanhood; we transcend the Ten Commandments and rise to that consciousness which Christ Jesus revealed in the two great commandments, which acknowledge but one power—one God, one Spirit, one Soul—and each and every one of us that same One.

Acknowledgment is only the first step. These commandments have to be lived. They have to be accepted in consciousness so that actually we learn how to forgive our enemies. We learn how not to criticize, judge, or condemn the person who has made a mistake, not to condone it, but in proportion as he seeks to rise above it to give that helping hand by perceiving the nature of God as the very Soul of every person. Any good human being can piously overlook the faults of others and even forgive them their sins. Any good human being can do that, but it takes spiritual vision to be able to say, "I cannot see anyone. The face of God is all that shines. The Soul of God looks out through all eyes."

Such a realization does not heal sick or sinning people: It makes them "die" more quickly so that their spiritual Self-hood can be revealed. The sooner mankind "dies" to his humanhood, the sooner will his Soul come forward and be revealed.

A well-known and wise man once asked me why I spent so much time doing healing work. For example, he wondered what good it would do for a very elderly woman to be healed because in a year or two she would pass on anyway and in the meantime what would she do with even a little good health: "What is she going to do with her healing—knit more booties for her grandchildren?"

While I understand that viewpoint, it is not my point of view. I have no interest in whether grandmothers knit booties for their grandchildren. I am interested only that the Soul of every person here on earth be revealed, the Soul that will remain here eternally. I am not interested in preaching to sinful people in an effort to make them good, nor even in giving sick people treatments so that they will become well. I recognize the place of all this in the ascending scale, but that is not the ultimate of our destiny. That is not the goal toward which we are working.

The time has come now, not to think in terms of being healthy or wealthy: The time has come to think in terms of being spiritual. The time has come to think of being, of having that Spirit of God indwelling so that we may claim our heritage as children of God, "joint-heirs with Christ" to all the heavenly riches. The time has come when we have to give thought to this: If we are crucified, can we rise from the tomb? If we are crucified, whether on the cross or through the calendar, can we rise and walk this very earth again in a physical body—speak, eat, and drink?

It must come to every single one of us that there is something more to life than being healthy and having abundance. There is something more to life than just walking around this earth enjoying ourselves. There is something more to life, and that is Life. Life is eternal, a Life that knows no grave, a Life that knows no infirmity, a Life that knows no sin, no poverty, no war, no lack. Can this Life be achieved?

Everyone who attains a tiny grain of spiritual vision can help in the attainment of this Life by healing the physical, mental, moral, and financial ills of his neighbor. We can help one another to a greater sense of abundance, and we can reveal spiritual truth and impart it, thereby helping our neighbor along the way. But that is as far as we can go.

After that, each one has to "die" within his own consciousness to the old man so that the new man can be born. Each one has to do that for himself by recognizing that it can be done and that there are those who have been on earth who have never died, and if we can rise high enough in consciousness, we can tabernacle with them.

There are those who hold communion right now with Christ Jesus, with Moses, Abraham, Lao-tse, Buddha, and John. Why not? We can commune with friends who are sitting beside us. "Ah," but you say, "my friends are alive." And so are these other great Souls. No man ever dies after he has had spiritual illumination. A single bit of realization that there is more to life than matter, more to life than meets the eye, even that is enough illumination to prevent one from ever dying. It takes only a grain of God-consciousness.

That does not necessarily mean that we will all walk the earth forever. That is not part of the plan. It was not meant that our children remain children forever. They have to become youths, adults, and finally attain maturity. There are different states and stages of consciousness, and no one of us remains in the same state forever. If every person reaching years of maturity would only realize that he has outgrown one stage of his life but to fit him for another, these middle and upper years of our life would be the most fruitful, the most joyous, the happiest, and the most prosperous of all.

There is within each one of us the Son of God. The Christ is not a man who walked the earth two thousand years ago. That man was Jesus, but the Christ is the Spirit of God in man. It was that Spirit which was the transcendental Consciousness of Jesus, and it is that transcendental Consciousness which is the Son of God in us. Its function is to heal disease, to feed, clothe, and house us, to be a protection, safety, and security unto us, even as it was in Galilee.

In order to avail ourselves of It, we must give up the God of reward and the God of punishment and accept a God of love in whom is no darkness—no human qualities, no traits of mortality. When we know God in this way and when we no longer fear God or his wrath or punishment and understand that God is love and God is life eternal, we shall know that we are not under any threat of disease, death, or old age because there is no provision in God for such things.

The function of the Master, that is, the Christ within us, is to nullify age, sinful thoughts and desires, disease, lack, limitation, and ultimately the last enemy, death itself. If we sow to the Spirit, if we abide in the spiritual truth that I and the Father are one, inseparable and indivisible, even if we make our bed in hell, or even if we walk through the valley of the shadow of death temporarily, I and my Father are still inseparable and indivisible. We are one, and all that the Father has is ours, not because we earn it or deserve it, but by the grace of God.

What God does, He does without any reason for doing it. Is God's love less than a mother's love? What a mother does for her child, she does without any reason: She does not ask for any return from the child. The mother knows that she is pouring herself forth for the child because of love. A mother never punishes her child—discipline, yes, but from a normal mother, punishment, no. Does a human mother love an erring child less than a good child? On the contrary, sometimes a little more. And does a mother know more of love than God? Is God less than a human mother?

God is not a superhuman being. God is not a person with human emotions. God does not pity and God does not condemn. God is, and God is available to all who can acknowledge that God is. All of our nonsensical prayers of beseeching God to be other than He is will stop once we realize that God is not influenced by man, nor does He take orders from man.

God does not accept our idea of what constitutes justice, love, and mercy, but God imparts to us His idea of justice, love, and mercy if we listen for the still small Voice. Let us honor God by realizing God's omnipotence, omniscience, and omnipresence. God is the infinite intelligence and love that maintains universal law. Instead of praying up to God, let us be so silent within ourselves that we can hear the still small Voice.

# CHAPTER III

# BEYOND POWER

As long as man has someone or something to which he can cling, he will not find God. Whatever man knows or is able to know with his human mentality—whether a thing or a thought—is not God. No one is going to find God while he has anything on which to stand, anything to which he can hold, or anything about which he can think. Startling and unbelievable as this may seem to be, nevertheless it is true.

Most of us have known a fair share of the good things of life and a few of the bad ones; and while we may not have been happy with the bad things, we undoubtedly would also admit that we did not find any permanent happiness in the good ones. Many of us must have suspected that there is something beyond all this, but what? What is that something? Is it God, and if so, what is it that men call God? Is God just a vague hope, a senseless dream, or is God really attainable? Is it possible to know God?

The search for God is not easy for anyone, and when the revelation of God does come, it is something so entirely different from what was expected that if a person is honest he will have to confess that it is beyond his understanding. Only after finding corroboration for what he himself has discovered as it is presented in a thousand different ways through the spoken and written word and then living with it for years and years, does it ultimately register.

Religions have evolved because somewhere far back in the past men were constantly encountering troubles of one sort or another in their human experience. If they were fishermen, they found that the fish were not running well in some seasons; if they were hunters, there were periods when the game was scarce; and for those engaged in farming, some years there was too much rain and some years not enough. Occasionally, there were enemies from across the border molesting them, and at such times the strong nearly always overcame the weak, plundering their less powerful neighbors and often reducing them to the status of slaves. Even if they did not hold their captives in complete physical slavery, they held them in mental slavery, keeping them in as much darkness as possible that they might exploit them the more easily; but then, if and when the weak became strong, the picture was often reversed.

The record of history indicates that the mighty have always taken from the weak. Bullets overpowered those who had bows and arrows; cannon triumphed over bullets; and finally bombs overcame cannon. One power has always been used to overcome another power, and as a last resort, men have turned to God hoping that He would be more powerful than the weapons they possessed.

The Old Testament is filled with accounts of people and nations who called upon God to destroy their enemies. That these enemies were more wicked than they and, therefore, deserved to be destroyed is usually not recounted—only that they needed the land of their enemies or their enemies' slaves, or that they needed some other thing which their enemies possessed. Their whole object in praying to God was that He would wipe out the enemy and deliver to them their property!

That is what God means to most people today—something to use. Only now, instead of being concerned merely with their human enemies, people have assigned to God the additional responsibility of removing their diseases and sins. Always man seeks a greater power with which to overcome those powers that disturb or annoy him.

Today, the world has witnessed the discovery of tremendous powers which are greater than any ever expected of, or attributed to, God because material powers have been discovered which can almost instantaneously wipe out the enemy if only the aggressor can get there first. The world has even discovered mental powers, but no one has yet discovered, either in the physical realm, the mental or the spiritual, a power that can destroy or overcome the sins, diseases, and poverty of the world.

This modern mechanistic world is still seeking exactly what it sought before the days of Abraham, Isaac, and Jacob; it is still praying to God for the same things for which our pagan ancestors prayed. Man has not yet learned the great lesson that the overcoming of any and every difficulty is not through using any kind of power; and if in all the thousands of years the world has not learned the folly of seeking powers with which to overcome error, it may be wise to let it pursue its vacillating course while we walk the high way, the infinite way, demonstrating that there are no powers to be overcome because life is to be lived "not by might, nor by power, but by my spirit."

When the great wizard of General Electric, Charles P. Steinmetz, said forty years ago that the next great discovery in the world would be spiritual power, he was prophetic. It must be understood, however, that this spiritual power to which he referred is not power in the commonly accepted meaning of the term: Spiritual power is the lack of power; it is no power in the sense that it is nothing that the world can conceive of as power because it is neither physical nor mental. It is not a power that can be manipulated by man, and that is why a term such as *using Truth* is archaic. Truth cannot be used. God cannot be used. Imagine man's using God! The very thought is shocking.

When spiritual power is finally understood, it will be revealed to be *no-power*. And what is the meaning of such a statement? No-power means a state of consciousness in which there are not two forces combating one another, there are not two powers, one to be used to destroy the other. In other words, there is not a spiritual power that can be used by anyone to destroy his enemies; there is no spiritual power that can be used in place of the nuclear power upon which the world is now relying.

Some of us may think that inasmuch as the power we are seeking and hoping to use is spiritual, that makes its use legitimate. But what we really are doing is expecting spiritual power to do exactly what we have relied upon bombs to do. Let us not be deluded into believing that it is possible to find some undiscovered power to do what the already discovered powers are failing to do. We are not going to find a spiritual power to destroy or overcome anything: Instead, we are going to overcome the belief that there is good or evil in any effect or in any form.

When I was led to meditate on this idea of power, I saw that the cause of all the turmoil and conflict in life lies in the deep-seated belief in two powers which has resulted in such attitudes as that of the survival of the fittest, self-preservation as the first law of nature, and the use of force in war and in almost every other activity of human existence. Always throughout the ages one power has been used to overcome, destroy, or replace another power, and yet despite all this use of power, the same evils that were on earth at the beginning of time are still plaguing the world. The passing of years has not in any sense eliminated or destroyed the power of evil.

It was in meditation, while pondering this, that the question came to my mind, "Does this mean that what man is searching for is a greater power to do something to these other powers? Is it possible that there is a spiritual force which will destroy material power and supplant it? And, in the event that such a spiritual force might be discovered, is there a possibility that some evils may develop in its use so that ultimately the world will have to find still another power with which to overcome the spiritual power? What is the limit? Where does it all stop?"

I knew that wherever power of any kind has been used there have always been the possibility and the potentiality of its being used either for good or for evil. "How can this be?" was the question I asked in my meditation. "In a God-ordained world, is it possible that God-power can be used for both good and evil?"

Quick as a flash the question answered itself: "No, if you ever discover what God-power is, you will learn that it has no opposite and no opposition; it cannot be used for good and it cannot be used for evil: It can only remain the creative, maintaining, and sustaining power of good, a power which cannot be used. God-power cannot be used: It can use us, but it cannot be used by us." That is the power the world awaits, a power which will prove to be no power, a power that no one can use, but that only God Itself* can express, activate, and motivate.

It became very clear to me that as long as there is a belief in two powers, there will be some people who will use power for good and other people who will use it for evil; but inasmuch as inertia prevents most members of the human family from taking a positive stand for good, the evil will usually predominate.

When power rested primarily on material force, there were both good and bad material forces operating. Then came

---

* In the spiritual literature of the world, the varying concepts of God are indicated by the use of such words as "Father," "Mother," "Soul," "Spirit," "Principle," "Love," and "Life." Therefore, in this book the author has used the pronouns "He" and "It" or "Himself" and "Itself" interchangeably in referring to God.

the era when mental power was in the preponderance, and for a short while it was a good era, during which time mental power was used for healing and regeneration, but it was not long before it was discovered that mental power could be used for evil purposes as well as for good. Today the world as always is a world of both material and mental forces. The challenge is to go beyond the use of any force or power to a state of no power.

For every bit of good power in the physical or mental realm that can be brought to bear in any situation, somebody in this world is going to discover how to use a corresponding amount of evil power. The ultimate solution to this battle of opposing forces is the ability to rise to God-power, which is not good power but a creative, maintaining, and sustaining power; to rise to a dimension of life in which there is no power, that is, no power that can be used.

In a God-created universe, the secret of life is no power. When we come to the place of no power, no power can operate against us, in us, or through us. That puts us in a very humble position where much as we may dislike doing it, we have to acknowledge as Jesus did, "I can of mine own self do nothing."

That is the goal of this message—to come to a place where we do not pay lip service to the statement, "I can of mine own self do nothing," but where we demonstrate that it is actually true and let whatever it is that is the power of God, the no-power, assert Itself and do the work.

There is a second part of this principle which is of equal importance and a natural corollary of the first part. I have stated that men have always sought for a power to overcome other powers, but they have also sought for something more than that. They have sought for a God who would give them things—food, clothing, housing.

Because the Master knew that, he cautioned his followers, "Take no thought for your life, what ye shall eat, or what ye shall drink; nor yet for your body, what ye shall put on." He knew that long before his day men had been seeking a God to give them food, clothing, housing, companion-ship, supply, good crops, good hunting, and good fishing; and even though his command was that they stop seeking after things, two thousand years later the world still goes to church to pray for the very things that the New Testament admon-ishes it not to pray for. Men are still seeking a God to give them *things*—and failing, just as they failed to find a God who would be an insuperable power to destroy their enemies.

When we give up seeking the power of God, we shall find the no-power which brings harmony into our lives. When we give up seeking things of God, we shall receive the great-est gift—God Itself. We shall receive God in consciousness, in our inner sanctuary or temple, in that secret place of the most High, which is found in no other place than within ourselves. The great lesson to be learned is that the goal is God-realization, and that not for any purpose.

To those who are thinking, "Should I not have health?" or, "Should I not have abundant supply?" my answer is, "I suppose so—I suppose so because the grace of God supplies us abundantly with everything of which we have need, even in what appears to be this human scene, but we do not have any power to *get* these things from God. When we have the actual conscious realization of God, pain, lack, and limitation fade away."

Unfortunately, there will still be people who are sick or poor. The poor are always with us—the poor in health, the poor in purse, and the poor in morals. With these, we share out of our abundance to the best of our ability. More than that we cannot do. We can never give them all they need or want. That is an impossibility because there is no end to what "man, whose breath is in his nostrils" needs or wants; but until a person realizes the futility of seeking things, he will not be fulfilled.

Why do we not stop searching for the power of God, stop looking for some thought or some truth that we think will make us well or prosperous, and acknowledge that of our own selves we can do nothing, and that nobody ever has discovered a power that destroys his enemies? Let us rest in the realization that all the evil of this world constitutes but the "arm of flesh" and let it pass from our experience—let it pass—not by pushing or forcing it out, but by *letting* it pass. Nothing is accomplished by struggling physically or mentally, because struggling only increases what seems to be an evil power in our experience. It is you and I who falsely entertain a sense of the power of sin, false appetite, disease, lack, or limitation, a sense of power which the thing itself, whatever it is, does not have; and that is why no power discovered in the physical, mental, or spiritual realm has ever been sufficient to remove any unwanted condition.

Every time that the thought comes to us, "I need this"; "I need that"; "I would like this"; "I would like that"; "I should have this"; "I should have that"; our answer must be, " 'Man shall not live by bread alone'—by effect, by creation—but by Spirit, the Creator." That must be a continuous realization until we have overcome our desire for anybody or anything that is in the external realm. We have to lose all desire for the visible in the realization that we live not by that which is visible but by that which is invisible, and then we shall find that the Infinite Invisible will produce in our experience the persons, things, circumstances, and conditions necessary to our daily life.

In the same way, every time we are tempted to think of some power—some negative, evil, erroneous power that apparently is dominating our life, rendering it futile and fruitless and which we want destroyed—let us smile at it as we realize, "No, I have no need of any power with which to overcome this discord. There is a God, even though I do not know what God is. I cannot know what God is because It is beyond the utmost comprehension of the human mind. If I could think something that I believed to be God, or Truth, I would ultimately find that that is not It." And so it would go on unto eternity until we come to the realization that if we can think It, It is not That.

How could anyone possibly believe that a thought of God in his mind could be God? That would surely be localizing and *finitizing* Him. The great Solomon realized fully that even the magnificent Temple he had built could not house God. Nothing is great enough to house God. Not all the world can house Him, and yet we build a little doghouse in our minds, or a pigeon coop, and think that God is there simply because we have changed His name to Mind, Life, or Love, trying to anchor Him in thought where we think we can hold onto Him. How foolish that is! How impossible it is to build a mentality big enough for that! Why, this whole universe of men is not big enough to embrace God!

Let us be satisfied to know that God is, and that there is evidence of that in the life all around us—in the law of like begetting like, in the abundance of love that there is in a world as loveless as this world sometimes seems to be, in the immeasurable beauty of a world where so much beauty is being destroyed continuously.

What God is, we do not know, but there are many, many ways in which to observe and witness the *is-ness* of God— not by knowing God, but by seeing the effects of God. We do not know how God functions, but in The Infinite Way we have discovered that God operates in Silence when thought is stilled and when the human sense of self is so humble that it really and truly believes that "I can of mine own self do nothing," and then has the patience to wait for God's glory to be revealed.

It is only those who are ready to give up all their concepts of God, to stop dreaming, thinking, and outlining, who in that complete surrender can let God reveal Itself:

God, I know not what You are, or even how to pray to You. I know not how to go in or how to come out; I know not what to pray for.

I cannot believe in the God that the world has accepted for I have seen the fruitlessness and frustration which follow such blind faith. I must find the God whom no man knoweth, the God that is, the one true God that created this universe in His own image and likeness—perfect, harmonious, and whole—and who maintains and sustains it in its infinite and eternal perfection. In such a God I can believe.

Reveal Yourself, Father; show me Your will. Never again will I dishonor You by trying to tell You what I need and then attempt to coerce You into delivering it. Never will I expect You to do my will or my bidding—to be my messenger boy.

I place my life, my hand, my being, and my body in Your keeping. Do with them what You will, Father. Take my sins, my fears, and my diseases; take my health, and my wealth; take it all. I ask only one gift—the gift of You, Yourself.*

We can come to this state of receptivity and respond to it only at the point of our readiness, and our readiness comes only when we have experimented with all the different forms of God that the world presents to us—the God of the religious world, the metaphysical God, the God we think we can use, the God that demonstrates things. Every kind of God we try, and only when we come to the end of trying are we ready for this surrender, ready to give up seeking a great power to destroy our enemies or to shower us with gifts. We give up the desire for that kind of a God, and we rest in this word, "God is. Thy grace is my sufficiency—not power, not might. Man shall not live by outer powers or outer things, but by the Word."

Long ago those of us who have delved into metaphysics lost our faith in material power and material means. Now when we take the next step of giving up our faith in mental means—mental powers and remedies—we come to the real God who can be experienced, but who can never be known with the mind and who cannot be used.

* The italicized portions of this book are spontaneous meditations which have come to the author during periods of uplifted consciousness and are not in any sense intended to be used as affirmations, denials, or formulas. They have been inserted in this book from time to time to serve as examples of the free flowing of the Spirit. As the reader practices the Presence, he, too, in his exalted moments, will receive ever new and fresh inspiration as the outpouring of the Spirit.

## PART TWO

# FROM THE UNREAL

# TO THE REAL

# CHAPTER IV

# WHO TOLD YOU?

The world can never rise above the idea of using one power over another and into the realm of no power until the mystery of Genesis is solved. In this first book of the Bible, are found two completely contradictory and conflicting records of creation: The first chapter is obviously the work of a mystic who had achieved complete union with God and who saw that this entire universe is Consciousness appearing as form; whereas subsequent chapters contain an account of the creation of mind.

The first record of creation is a revelation of the activity of Consciousness in all its purity and eternality. It recounts the unfolding of a spiritual universe where there is light before there is a sun or a moon, where the crops are in the ground before the seeds are planted, and where there is man before there is woman. That which is formed of Consciousness is never born: It is merely an emanation of Consciousness, which not only has no beginning but has no ending because as long as there is Consciousness, there is Consciousness formed. When Consciousness appears as form, it can appear

53

as a seed or as a completely developed tree without ever having gone through any process of growth.

Consciousness, or Soul, which we call God, reveals and expresses Itself as a spiritual universe in which there is no conception and no birth. In other words, creation is the immaculate conception of God revealing Itself as individual identity, an identity expressing as human, animal, vegetable, and mineral forms; so that in reality, God, Consciousness, is the very essence and substance of the earth—even of what appears as stones, rocks, sand, and soil—just as that same Consciousness is the substance of our true identity.

In Genesis, we learn that God created Adam and Eve and placed them in the Garden of Eden in the midst of perfection and harmony, surrounded only by goodness, love, and beauty. Joy and harmony reigned there until into that Eden came something that destroyed it and ejected Adam and Eve from the Garden. That something has always remained more or less of an enigma, and yet the whole mystery is clearly explained in the second and third chapters of Genesis.

In the Garden of Eden, Adam and Eve were naked, but they were unaware of their nakedness; they had bodies but as long as they were of a pure mind, there was no shame in them—bodies were just normal, natural things, so why be ashamed of them? Yet the next thing we read is that Adam and Eve were ashamed because they knew they were naked. Suddenly the belief of evil had come into their minds, and they began to cover up and hide. What were they covering up and from what were they hiding except the belief of evil in their minds?

And God said to Adam, "Who told thee that thou wast naked?"

In that query is summed up the whole essence of human life. All of us are in that same predicament in which Adam found himself. As long as we entertain a belief of good and evil, we are the Adam who is hiding, the Adam who is outside the Garden of Eden, and because of that we are all covering up our "nakedness."

Everybody is hiding, hiding from someone or from himself, or hiding something within himself for fear of having it brought to light. Why? Because he is dwelling in the realm of good and evil. Who told him that this is good and that is bad? Who told him that it is more moral to cover up the body than to expose it? Who told him that there is sin? Who made this condition? From his very question, God certainly implies that He did not. God did not say there was anything wrong about a naked body, nor did He say there was anything wrong on the face of the earth.

The sin that crept into Eden was not an apple nor was it sex, although traditional religious opinion would so identify it. The sin was the acceptance of two powers; and, when man began to eat of the tree of the knowledge of good and evil, he took upon himself a dual universe so that no longer could it be said that he was too pure to behold iniquity, because now he saw and knew both good and evil.

The second chapter of Genesis departs radically from the first in that it is the account of the creation of mind, mind producing mental images—not externalized reality but mental images in thought—mind appearing as thoughts, changeable as the weather, thoughts which never penetrate beyond the realm of mind into the realm of being.

The truth of the matter is that neither thinking two times two is four, nor thinking two times two is not four will make it so. Two times two is four, *is* four, *is* four, *is*. It has nothing to do with thought. It would be so even if we did not think it so, because it *is*. Thinking cannot make anything true; but in the inner Silence, which is a listening attitude in which we are taught of God and in which God utters His voice, the earth melts—sin, sickness, and all lack disappear—and God imparts to us that which is. Only in the realm of being are we outside of thoughts where *IS*, is.

Who is there who has not had good thoughts and who is there who has not had evil thoughts? Who is there who has not had pleasant and unpleasant thoughts, healthy and sickly thoughts, pure thoughts and sinful thoughts? That is because thoughts that emanate solely from the mind are always either good or evil.

This mental creation is not a creation of Spirit, or Consciousness, but a creation of the false or carnal mind, a mind that is constituted of both good and evil, that thinks correctly and incorrectly, having no Consciousness, or God, for its guide. The entire sense-world, made up of that which we see, hear, taste, touch, and smell, has no existence whatsoever except as a creation of this carnal mind which by its very nature and from its very inception is finite, unreal, and unstable with nothing to support it except thoughts which shift from good to evil, and from evil back to good.

The very moment that we recognize that the second chapter of Genesis describes mind in action, we have the secret of its destruction: Rise above mind, above thought. God's thoughts are not our thoughts. We do not have the capacity to think God's thoughts, but when the mind, in rising above thought, has been transcended and Silence supersedes thought, God can utter His word through us.

When we are able to rise above the realm of thought to that high place where we have no opinion whether anything or anybody is good or evil, but are willing to be a perfect transparency for the instruction of God, then God speaks in our ear and shows us the spiritual reality which exists right where that "man of flesh" who "cannot please God" appears to be; but in that instant when God speaks, the man of flesh is transformed into the Son of God and is immediately returned to the Garden of Eden where he is now the Son of God living under God's government.

The belief in two powers is what traps us into vacillating between the pairs of opposites—harmony and discord, poverty and abundance, life and death, sickness and health; whereas the ability to abide in our inner being, realizing that there is only one power—that there is no good and there is no evil in any form—frees us and brings the peace that passes understanding.

The only devil is the knowledge of good and evil. We

decide that this is good and it is so unto us, or that this is evil and so it is; whereas the truth is that "there is nothing either good or bad, but thinking makes it so." Then to be rid of the pairs of opposites, we must stop the merry-go-round of the human mind, and that actually is not as difficult or as impractical as it sounds.

I have been asked many times, "How do you stop thinking?" And I have found one way. The minute I can look at any person or condition and know that it is neither good nor evil, my thought stops, and my mind becomes quiet. That is the end of it because then there are no thoughts left for me to think about it: I do not think good of it and I do not think evil of it. All I know is that *it is*, and then I am back at the center of my being where all power is. Our mind is restless only when we are thinking about things or persons, either in terms of good or evil, but the mind is at rest when we surrender all such concepts.

After we have had enough experience hitting up against every form of error that can conceivably come to the human race and have seen at least a portion of it rendered a nothingness just by realizing that there is neither good nor evil because there is only God, then we are approaching the place where eventually we may have sufficient conviction to respond to our particular Pilate as did Jesus to his, "Thou couldest have no power at all against me, except it were given thee from above."

Throughout my years of healing work, I have learned that if I can be made to accept the condition or the person that is brought to me as either good or evil, just in that proportion will I fail to bring forth a healing. Healing comes with the realization, "This is not evil and this is not good; there is neither good nor evil here because God is here, and where God is, 'where the Spirit of the Lord is, there is liberty.'"

When we lived in Eden, that is, in harmony and perfection as pure offspring of God, we were as gods—complete and whole—and the way to return to the Garden of Eden is to give up the pairs of opposites. Complete harmony comes when we no longer desire good any more than we desire evil, because when we desire anything, although we may think we are desiring good, actually we have not the least way of knowing whether our fulfilled desire will result in blessing or harm. Even as apparently a desirable and much sought after thing as having a million dollars can be harmful and destructive, as many people have discovered to their sorrow.

Traditional metaphysical teaching would agree that we must rise above evil, but it still looks longingly toward good, hoping to see the evil translated into good, and that is where it makes the mistake which results in the inability to attain the final harmony.

As long as we can be made to believe that one thing is good and another evil, we shall remain outside the Garden of Eden, and one day have health and another day disease, experience youth and vitality one day and age and debility another day because those are the pairs of opposites and they follow one another in cycles. It is only when we do not desire wealth or harmony any more than lack or discord, but seek only that which was original and primary in the Garden of Eden, that we rise above these opposites into eternal life. In this state of consciousness, we are pure enough to dwell in the Garden of Eden which is a state of desirelessness—a contentedness with being.

The original purity of Adam and Eve consisted of this desirelessness. They were constituted of God and given all that they needed by the grace of God: God was their being; God was their life; God even formed and governed their body. All day long they enjoyed the good things of life, until into the midst of this paradise, good and evil entered their consciousness, after which they no longer walked blissfully up and down the Garden, but walked right out of Eden into the world where they became the man and woman of earth. They turned from the sheer joy of *being* into that state of consciousness in which they had to earn their living by the sweat of their brow—by their mind—and bring forth children in pain.

As long as we have a knowledge of good and evil, we too are living in the world like that of Adam and Eve who were expelled from the Garden of Eden, and we are subject to chance and change, to accident, limitation, and old age.

In the eighth chapter of Romans, we read that "the man of flesh," that is, the Adam-man, cannot please God, is not under the law of God, and is only the child of God if so be that the Spirit of God dwell in him. Let us never forget, however, that there are not two of us. There is not a real man and an unreal man; there is not a real universe and an unreal universe. There is only one universe and that is the real universe; there is only one you and that is the real you. Actually, the man of flesh is that real man even before the Spirit of God has been awakened in him because the first Adam and the last Adam are both spiritual—the one, pure before he is expelled from Eden, and the other, pure after his return.

So it is that you and I are that pure child of God, born into Eden, but at this moment entertaining a sense of good and evil. We are moving about as the man and woman of flesh who cannot please God and cannot be under the law of God, until at some given time in our lives it is revealed to us that the whole difference between the original Adam and Eve, the God-created, pure, eternal being, and you and me as we now are is that we know good and evil.

If we want to return to the Edenic state and be the man and woman we were in the beginning—the pure creation—all we have to do is give up our knowledge of good and evil. In reality, such knowledge is all in the realm of theory, belief, or human concepts. We must be willing to look upon all the good as well as the evil conditions in our life and in the world, and state with conviction, "I renounce you, both of you. Henceforth, I know neither good nor evil; I know only God manifest. Through spiritual vision, I behold Consciousness forming Itself in immortal forms—eternal, harmonious, and abundant. Henceforth, I accept only the revelation of the real creation in which there is light even when there is no sun and where all is harmony."

There is no other way, and whether or not we are willing to accept this idea, the secret of harmonious living lies in the ability to withdraw all our estimates and judgments of situations and people. It is difficult to do this because at first we have to live a dual life. For example, it is unavoidable that we be aware of evil in the world—evil conditions and at times evil men. There is not any doubt but that like the Master we may have to whip those evil ones occupying important governmental posts out of the temple by voting against them and exposing corruption in high places, although all this must be done with as much detachment as that of an actor who plays a part on the stage. In the play, his role may be that of a thief who has stolen a million dollars, but the crime perpetrated in the play will not benefit or harm him because he has only been playing a part and going through the motions required of the character. An actor does not have to be a villain to play the part of one—he merely has to act like one, and as soon as his curtain call has been taken, he removes his make-up and is his own self again.

So it is with us. We say and do things in this state of dualism in which we live, but we must learn to smile an unbelieving smile within ourselves because we remember that we are only actors in a play and, therefore, do not accept appearances at appearance-value.

True, we have to rebuke evil: Sometimes we have to vote against it; sometimes we have to talk against it; and sometimes we have to correct children and even grownups too. But this has to be done without our actually believing it, recognizing, "Yes, that's the appearance-world, and the people in it have not awakened to this great secret that there is neither good nor evil in person, place, or thing."

We have to be able to look around at a roomful of people with a silent agreement, "I know that there is not an evil person in this room, not an evil thought, not a thief, not a liar among all of them." But that is not enough: We have to go a little bit further and add, "But neither is there a good one."

In our early days in metaphysics, it was difficult for many of us to unsee evil, but it is far more difficult to reach that high state of consciousness in which we are able to rise above good—above good health and good supply—and retire into a realm of consciousness where even though outwardly we are living a normal life, inwardly is the conviction, "I will not accept appearances; I will not accept them. I stand on IS. God is and only God is: There cannot be bad conditions and there cannot be good conditions. There can only be God."

The first chapter of Genesis is the account of a spiritual universe, peopled by spiritual beings who do not live by effect but by cause, who do not live by bread alone, who do not have to earn their living by the sweat of their brow; whereas in the second and third chapters, a knowledge of good and evil creates a sense of separation from God after which man lives by power and by effect: He lives by bread, by money, by the beating of the heart, by sunlight; he lives by all the creature things, instead of by the Creator.

At the present moment of reading, this may not seem too hard to accept because, if we have renounced and forsaken both good and evil, we are now pure, immortal, eternal being, without sin and unashamed, knowing there is nothing at all to fear because we are living by God's grace; but let us not forget that tomorrow there will be problems that will tend to throw us right outside the Garden of Eden; tomorrow there will be mail and telephone calls which will tempt us to be hypnotized by the appearance of good and evil.

When these moments come, let us remember that that is when fortitude is required, but that is also when the grace of God comes forward to enable us to stand fast in our spiritual integrity.

The truth that there is neither good nor evil in any form is the secret of no-power; it is the secret of life for which people have sought throughout the ages. They have called it a search for God, for the Holy Grail, but when they found it, if they did, what they found was that there is neither good nor evil in effect. When they discovered that secret, they had their foot right inside of heaven, because they had found the ultimate reality. It is only the knowledge of good and evil that keeps anyone from the holy kingdom.

# CHAPTER V

# TRANSCENDING MIND

In the beginning, there was only one state of consciousness, the spiritual, but ever since the so-called Fall, man has been divided into three states of consciousness—the material, mental, and spiritual. Spiritual consciousness, when made flesh, is the perfect, immortal body, but few of all the billions of people who have lived on this planet have achieved spiritual consciousness, very few. Instead, throughout countless generations of humanhood, the world has been living in a material and mental state of consciousness, and for the most part, all that has been known is a material sense of the world, a world in which men make their living by the sweat of their brow and in which everything they do is done by physical or mental means.

Even today the world has not risen too far above that physical sense of a universe, despite the fact that in this last century more of the mental has been revealed, although revealed primarily in the sense of the mental governing the physical. Out of that has come what is known as the science of right thinking, designed to manipulate the human scene.

For example, if a person does not have a home, all he has to do is to catch hold of the right thought and the home appears, or if he does not have a satisfactory companion, just a little right thinking, and the old companion vanishes and a new one appears! If he suffers from some physical discord, just a little bit of right thinking, holding the "right thoughts," and lo and behold, the diseased body disappears and the harmonious body appears in its place.

Even when this sort of mental therapy is effective, and it often is, those using this technique are still left with a physical universe—a physical body, a physical companion, a physical anything subject to the laws of good and evil—and the very next day it is possible for the discords and inharmonies to begin all over again. One part of the body is healed, and then another one speaks up; the problem of supply is solved, and something else pops up; and so it goes from one belief of physical, mental, moral, or financial inharmony to another, and always there is the same attempt to use the power of the mind to adjust, heal, or improve the condition.

Nevertheless, the world is fortunate to have made even that much progress, because without the revelation of the mental realm, it would have been almost impossible to take the next higher step into the spiritual kingdom.

Before we proceed any further, let us understand the function of the mind. Perhaps this can best be done by using the body as an example. Everybody is aware that the body is an instrument used for the activity of human life, but few people recognize that because it is an instrument of God it should be perfectly harmonious. There is no reason why the body should deteriorate or lose its faculties, and it appears to do so only because man has not yet learned how to prevent such changes and maintain the body so that it is a proper and effective instrument for daily use. This can be done by realizing that the mind also is an instrument and that it, too, has its rightful place in our human experience.

When it is understood that the mind is an instrument, it should also be understood of what it is the instrument, because an instrument must of necessity have something governing and controlling it. Unfortunately, the average mind is not controlled, even though some people try to control it, thereby often working havoc with their lives because they have not yet learned that the mind cannot be controlled by man.

The mind is an instrument for something higher than itself, and that something is the one Self. When we come to the point where the mind is governed by the Self, we will be embraced in a peace that passes understanding. Then we do not control the body or the mind, but the activity of Truth in our consciousness, of which we become aware through the mind, keeps the mind clear, clean, harmonious, and vital; and it in its turn manages, controls, and governs the body, acting as the purifying agent of both mind and body.

There is a spiritual center within every one of us, and in that center is stored up our entire spiritual heritage. This center is not within the body, but in our consciousness, and we can draw out of the infinity of our consciousness all that is necessary for our unfoldment from this day unto the end of the world and beyond it into infinity.

The original and basic creative principle and substance of life is God, Soul, or Consciousness, but mind is the instrument through which God's activity takes place, because properly understood and utilized, mind is an instrument of God. When the mind is open to receive the divine Impulse, harmonious and perfect form flows out from it.

Through Adam, the mind of man accepted a belief of good and evil, and from that moment on, instead of being a pure instrument of the Soul, mind began forming itself in material forms of both good and evil, just as if it were a mold similar to a muffin tin—whatever the shape of the muffin tin, that is the shape in which the muffins come out. Similarly, the product of mind appears as form. If there is evil in the mind, it appears as evil form, and contrariwise, if there is good in the mind, it appears as good form.

The mind produces its own image and likeness, and if we

who stand behind the mind permit it to be filled with superstition, ignorance, or fear, all of which stem from the belief in two powers, that is what the mind produces in our experience. Mind is the substance of every form of sin, disease, death, false appetite, lack, limitation, wars, rumors of wars, and all the other things listed under the word *evil*.

A mind filled with evil thoughts—fear, hate, injustice, lust, or malice—must appear outwardly as inharmony and discord; whereas a mind filled with good thoughts—charity, purity, benevolence, or co-operation—must appear outwardly as the good life. That is the karmic law as taught in Scripture: "Whatsoever a man soweth, that shall he also reap." The mind in its unillumined state, filled with materialistic beliefs, theories, opinions, doctrines, and creeds can only manifest its own state of chaos; but a mind freed of these beliefs becomes the instrument through which the creative Principle of life can flow as harmonious and eternal form. *The external appearance is always mind-formed.* As we sow mentally, so shall we reap materially.

Matter is matter only to the material state of consciousness, but once we rise to a mental state of consciousness, matter is not matter, but mind. Mind is the essence and substance of which matter is formed, and it appears to us as form or effect. Mind is the principle, the life and the law, of all material and mental form.

This is not an easy concept to grasp, but if we draw an analogy between this and a substance with which we are all familiar, it may clarify the idea. The combination of two parts hydrogen and one part oxygen is called water, but water can be changed into steam or into ice, and whether this particular substance appears as water, steam, or ice, it is just a different form of one essence—two parts hydrogen and one part oxygen.

In this same manner, mind is the basic substance, but matter is the name given to mind when it takes form. Mind appears as many forms: Flesh is one of them, blood is another, bone another, and hair yet another; but every one of these is mind made visible, mind appearing as specific form. Mind in one form is flesh and in another it is bone, gristle, blood, hair, or skin; but always the substance, or essence, is mind.

Mind functions as thought; mind appears as thing; and on this level, mind is the essence of creation as described in the second and third chapters of Genesis. Therefore, if matter is mind, a process of mind can change the product, matter.

Mind—your mind and my mind—imbued with spiritual truth becomes the instrument through which God appears, in and through which God manifests, and God appearing becomes the body of our outer world. Therefore, never do we live in a material world with material surroundings because God, Itself—Truth in your consciousness and my consciousness—is the very substance and essence of our world.

When God, or Soul, becomes the activity of the mind and appears as form, then all form is spiritual and can be multiplied. When we rise above the level of mind and thought to the Silence, that is where I, God, becomes the activity and substance appearing as matter or form. For example, in every miracle in the four Gospels, it was the mind of Jesus Christ which appeared outwardly as health and harmony and as an infinity of loaves and fishes. Loaves and fishes are not matter; health and wealth are not matter: They are mind formed. Once the mind becomes permeated with truth, truth becomes the substance and the essence of all form, and then the form can be multiplied, but it can be multiplied only because it is not matter.

There was a time when there were only one billion people on earth. Now there are four billion, but no more of God is on earth. The same God is here, the same life is here, but what has happened is that *mind has multiplied form, not divided it.* This is the same principle that was in operation when Jesus performed the miracle of the loaves and fishes. What he did was to multiply the visible form to satisfy the sense of need at that particular moment.

There is only Spirit and its spiritual formations; but mind, as the instrument of Spirit, forms and governs itself as out-lined form, and this is called matter or physical form. Ac-tually, it is mind, because matter can be reduced to the mental and eventually back into the spiritual; but mind *appears* to us as finite forms, and it is mind that forms that form. Mind will even transform this body and provide for it. Mind will form for us everything of which we seem to have need—and yet no new thing will have been added to creation.

Mind, when it functions on its own level, appears as either good or evil, or both; whereas mind when functioned by Soul or God appears only as a harmonious universe. This does not mean that when we think good thoughts, our per-fect spiritual universe appears; it means that when we have risen above both mind and thought into the realm of Silence, Soul or God now manifests as our spiritual identity, being, body, and universe.

When you and I permit our minds to be filled with igno-rance, superstition, and selfishness, that mind produces its own image and likeness, which is mirrored forth as the sins and diseases of the world; but when the mind is purified, so that it becomes an instrument for the pure Soul, then the mind produces the image and likeness of the Soul which is "according to the pattern shewed to thee in the mount"—spiritual perfection.

The creations of God are incorporeal, spiritual, and infinite, not physical, material, or finite. God is Spirit, and therefore the universe of God and the body of God are spiritual. How-ever, as the creations of God present themselves to our hu-man sense, they appear to be physical, material, and limited. The reason for this anomaly is that our mind in its unillu-mined state is interpreting to us only what we can become aware of through our senses. We do not behold what *is*: We behold the interpretation of our mind.

For example, if there were a bowl of yellow roses in the room, you and almost everyone in the room would see them as yellow; but to the person who is color-blind, they might be interpreted as some other color; or, while these same roses might be beautiful to you, they might precipitate an attack of rose fever or asthma in another person. Clearly, it is not what we become aware of that is important, but *how the mind interprets that of which we are aware.*

There are artists whose interpretation of roses might startle us because they are able to perceive some underlying spiritual truth about them, whereas we see only their finite physical form and color. Some of us might visit an art gallery, look at masterpieces, and call them daubs of paint; and yet others could look at the same pieces of canvas and live in an ecstasy because through their developed understanding of art, their knowledge of line and color, they could appreciate and see what the artist saw when he put his vision on canvas. If we have developed any appreciation in the field of art, then we can stand before the artist's canvas fully aware of what he has placed there; but if our mind has no knowledge of art, we would then see nothing but splotches of paint.

When our mind is free of judgments, we can look out at this world and enjoy the sky, the air, the earth, the oceans, the sun, moon, and stars, but if our mind is filled with material concepts, we shall query as a friend of mine did years ago, "I don't see why people travel. There are only two kinds of earth—it goes up and they call it mountains; it goes down and they call it valleys. Or it is wet and they call it water. Now what can anyone see in travel? What difference is there between one place and another?"

We rarely see what is before us. Everything that we observe in the world, we see through the eyes of our background —our parents' attitude toward life, our racial and religious roots, our national heritage, our early environment, our education, and then later the experiences that we garner after leaving school.

These concepts are formed by prenatal influence, early environment, education, and personal experience, which make of you and me what we are—human beings. So it is that if our world is a world of harsh, bitter, and disagreeable people, it sometimes is because those four factors have conditioned us and influenced our interpretation of what we encounter. On the other hand, if we are meeting with a world of co-operative, understanding, and loving people, that, too, is probably due to our particular frame of reference.

Right where we are is the very kingdom of God. All that is in heaven is on earth; but whether we find earth a heaven or a hell depends upon whether we are seeing the earth through spiritual or through material vision. The mind's interpretation of experience determines whether it is heaven or hell.

We look at the creations of God through the instrument of the mind, and the forms we see take on the color and complexion of the mind interpreting them. When a person comes to us and says, "I have a diseased body" or "I have a sick mind" or "I have an empty pocketbook," he is beholding creation through limited, finite, material sense; but if we can ignore what the person is seeing, feeling, and experiencing and realize that our mind is but an interpreter and if we can become sufficiently still so that the true picture can register, then out of the Silence we may hear, "Thou art my child, my beloved child, in whom I am well pleased" or "This very place is the kingdom of God" or "All that I have is thine." In other words, there comes an assurance from within that the scene, as mortal sense interprets it, is incorrect; and in the Silence what is actually there is revealed to us.

A person struggling with a problem is judging by appearances, and his mind is interpreting his world in the light of prenatal conditioning, environment, education, and later, personal experiences; whereas, when the mind interprets the scene through the pure activity of Soul, all judgment is set aside while we wait in the Silence, "Father, I have no judgment. I await Your judgment." And in such humility, spiritual vision illumines the scene.

In the human scene, the mind is creative. It can create good and it can create evil—and does. In the spiritual scene, however, the mind is not a creative faculty, but an avenue of awareness. For example, if we had a blank canvas in front of us and if instead of racking our brains as to what to put on it, we learned how to be still and waited, taking the attitude, "Here is a canvas. Father, You paint the picture," we would find ideas flowing freely, and into our consciousness would come the directions which our mind and hands would execute.

In such a state of receptivity, inventions, discoveries, plans on the trestle board, or whatever idea is necessary would unfold, and the ability would be given us to carry these ideas into execution. That is because the real seat of intelligence is Soul or Spirit, and divine Intelligence functions through Its instrument, the mind. The whole secret lies in making the transition from a thinking, plotting, planning, scheming mind to a mind at rest in a state of awareness, through which divine ideas can flow.

Ever since that illusory experience known as the Fall of man, however, mind has been used as a creative faculty, and that is what is at the root of our troubles and problems today. Therefore, when called upon to help our family, friends, or others, or even when in need of help ourselves, instead of trying to change the person or condition or instead of condemning ourselves or others, we should realize that this is just another form of mind presenting itself to us. The healing agency lies in our realization that *mind is not a power: Mind is an avenue of awareness.*

We can watch how miraculously this works whenever we are tempted with any form of error—whatever it may be—if we do not fight it, but quietly realize:

*God is the great and only creative principle of life, the source of all being. God alone! "Thou shalt have no other gods before me"—no other power, no other creator but One. God alone is, and this that is troubling me cannot be of God, so it must be of mind. It is mind presenting a picture to me of a lack of some kind.*

Those who live in the Spirit have flashes of the real or spiritual creation and are able to discern the real man made in

God's image and likeness, and to see that nothing has ever interfered with the harmony of the development and unfoldment of spiritual man.

On the human level, however, mind governs our body and all creation, and it governs it for both good and evil. It gives us health one day, and sickness another day; it gives us wealth one day, and lack the next day because the mind, being of the earth, earthy, is made up of the two qualities of good and evil, and therefore it manifests and expresses itself as these extremes. Until we rise above mind, we cannot rise above the pairs of opposites.

When we transcend mind and touch the realm of Spirit, we live in a different consciousness. No longer do we resort to the use of affirmations or denials, physical or mental remedies: Now we contact that spiritual center where we find peace, and then we find that we have transcended the activity of mind both as to good and evil and are living what the world calls a normal life, but which in reality is a spiritual life, a life that to a great extent is untouched by the activity of the unillumined mind.

Correctly understood, mind is an instrument of God, created by God. Therefore, mind itself is an effect, just as the product of mind is an effect. It is not a cause; it is an effect. God, Soul, Spirit alone is cause, and both mind and body are effects.

If we dwell with spiritual truth in our consciousness, none of the evils of this world will come nigh our dwelling place because the truth entertained in consciousness takes over and begins to live our lives. Living in an atmosphere of spiritual wisdom and feeding consciousness with truth, there comes a moment when that truth takes over the mind, and then no longer is it necessary to fill the mind with truth. From then on, the flow is the other way. It is not we who are thinking truth, remembering, declaring, or meditating on truth: It is Truth using our mind for Its expression, always using us, always flowing through us.

# CHAPTER VI

# UNCONDITIONED MIND

The basic secret of mind is that there is only one mind, and that mind is the mind of individual being—your mind and my mind. The implications of this profound statement have never been fully understood. The world at large does not know this, although it has been known to metaphysicians of all schools. When it has come to actual practice, however, an entity separate and apart from the one mind called mortal mind or the human mind has always been introduced and accepted as a power.

Actually, there is only one mind, and this mind is unconditioned: It has no qualities of good or of evil; it is a state of being, not good and not bad. In reality, there cannot be intelligent mind and ignorant mind; there cannot be healthy mind and diseased mind, for mind is unconditioned. Furthermore, mind forming itself as body is unconditioned; and therefore body is neither well nor sick, tall nor short, thin nor fat. Body is as unconditioned as the mind which is the essence of its form. Mind and body, being unconditioned, are a state of absolute being and perfection until the belief of good and evil is accepted into thought.

Human experience is *in reality* the perfect mind, your mind and my mind, which manifests as perfect being and body, but which as human experience is influenced by the knowledge of good and evil. This belief in two powers is the essence of what is called the carnal mind. To return to the Father's house and once more become the son of God, it is necessary that we individually—for no one can do this for us because it is an individual experience—give up the belief in good and evil through an activity of our consciousness.

Mind forms its own conditions of matter, body, and form. Mind does not *create*; mind *forms*. Creation is already complete—spiritual, eternal, and perfect—but our mind, depending on its conditioning, forms and interprets our human experience on this plane. If our mind is completely free of the judgment of good and evil, then Spirit forms its own image and likeness through the mind as happy, harmonious, and successful living. If mind is conditioned by judgments of good and evil, mind is not a clear transparency, and in proportion to its conditioning will experiences of good and evil take place in our lives.

Mind, when free of theories, superstitions, beliefs, and false concepts, governs material form harmoniously and eternally. If we had no false concepts of anything in this world, that is, no judgment whether anything is good or evil, we would soon discover that our mind would bring all forms to us— forms wondrous in their intricacy, beauty, and abundance. Only as we ourselves let the judgment of good or evil, healthy or unhealthy, operate, does the mind present those forms to us for our acceptance.

When the mind receives the light of spiritual wisdom, the appearance conforms more nearly to mind's pure form. As Soul governs Its spiritual activity and form, so mind, when it is free of hypnotism, that is, the belief of good and evil, receives the full light of Soul.

Mind, imbued with spiritual truth, is a law of renewal, regeneration, restoration, and resurrection. Your mind and mine, imbued with Truth, is the mind of those who come to us and of those embraced in our consciousness. Your mind and my mind imbued with Truth is the mind of individual being.

Anyone who has ever been the means of a spiritual healing knows that this is true and that his individual mind, as it is imbued with Truth, becomes a law of renewal, regeneration, or reformation expressing as physical, mental, moral, or financial healing to those who come to him.

As troubled people bring their problems to us, if we are able to see the person or condition as neither good nor evil, sick nor well, rich nor poor, that is, see him without judgment, we then no longer have a carnal mind, but are in full possession of the mind which was in Christ Jesus—a mind which recognizes only one power, an unconditioned mind—and it dispels the illusions of sense. We do not have to get rid of or overcome the carnal mind; we do not have to destroy it: We only have to understand that our mind is a perfect instrument for the Soul, and this it becomes as we fill our mind with spiritual truth and grace.

When we are faced with a problem at any level, we must first remember that the substance of the visible universe is unconditioned mind which is the instrument of pure, immortal Being, Essence, Substance, and Reality, and its formations are also unconditioned, because they are mind itself appearing as infinite form.

Mind, unconditioned and having no qualities of good or evil, is the substance of all that is visible; and all that is, is as unconditioned as the mind which is its basis. If this were not true, it would be impossible for our state of consciousness to produce changes in what is called the material universe. Those who have actually witnessed or experienced metaphysical and spiritual healing know that a practitioner may be anywhere from one to twenty-five thousand miles away from the patient and nevertheless be the instrument through which a fever is reduced, a lump removed, or wasted lungs restored, because when the practitioner has attained a sufficient stillness for the mind to be a pure transparency for God, the condition of the body changes.

Our consciousness of this truth is the law of harmony; and therefore if we were called upon to help someone who had a fever and were to realize that mind, *unconditioned mind*, is the substance of all visible form, and that this universal belief in two powers, good and evil, is not operative because it is the "arm of flesh," or nothingness, and then the fever disappeared, we would know that our consciousness of one power, which really is a consciousness of no-power, had produced the healing and was a law of harmony. We would observe that our mind functioning as an instrument of God had produced an effect on what we call body or matter and we would know then that the substance of mind and the substance of matter are one and the same. That is why mind can affect matter and, moreover, that is why truth in consciousness can affect matter.

Mind, itself, is unconditioned, but the human race has accepted the belief of both good and evil, and has produced a good effect by taking good into its mind and an evil effect by taking evil into its mind.

Mind, unconditioned—infinite, eternal mind—is the substance of being, body, business, politics, government, industry, finance, art, and literature. This mind and its formations are neither good nor bad: They are unconditioned eternal being, and that which we behold as an erroneous condition or circumstance is not of mind or its formations, but is the universal belief in good and evil, which is termed devil or carnal mind.

Actually, there is no such thing as carnal mind, because there is but one mind and it is unconditioned. It is not mortal, it is not human; it cannot be named, described, or analyzed. That which we call carnal mind is merely a *belief* in two powers, and when you recognize that, you can stop fighting error or trying to overcome it, rise above it, or remove it. Never try to protect yourself from mortal mind or carnal mind. The nature of any protective work must be your realization that there are not two powers, and all you ever have to protect yourself from is that belief in two powers.

As you begin to perceive that mind is unconditioned, your thoughts never turn to the subject of good or evil. You are just living each circumstance of life as it comes along. This does not mean withdrawing from the world: It means being in the world but not of it, living each experience without trying to cling to it if it seems good or without trying to get rid of it if it seems evil. It is a life of nonattachment to things. It is only when we are trying to cling to something or to somebody or trying to get rid of someone or some condition that we are attached.

The moment that you think of mind in terms of your mind and my mind, separate and apart from the one unconditioned mind, you have missed the point; but once you begin to understand that there is only one mind, you will never do anything unless it is in keeping with God's law. It will never be your will or my will: It will be God's will.

In the surrender of personal will, this unconditioned mind can operate in us and through us. As long as we condition mind with beliefs of good and evil, we will bring forth good and evil in proportion to our faith or belief. As a man becomes convinced in his heart, so is it unto him. It is all a matter of conditioning, and you can condition yourself for good or for evil; but when you leave the realm of conditioning, you are in the realm of that mind which was also in Christ Jesus.

In all the healings that Jesus brought forth in his ministry, it was the Father's will that was being performed through him, and he knew that it was not his mind, but the Father's mind: It was the unconditioned mind. Therefore, he could say to a blind man, "Open your eyes." He could say to the crippled man, "What did hinder you?" In other words, there was no conditioned condition in his consciousness. There was only unconditioned mind which is neither healthy nor sick, neither rich nor poor.

This is truth, but you can make it truth in your experience only by applying it to every appearance that faces you—on the street, at home, in school, in the factory, or in the

market—always keeping before you the truth that unconditioned mind is formed as unconditioned effect.

Spiritual wisdom must be made tangible. It must bear
fruit in our earthly experience, but this it cannot do if we
do not become consciously aware of it. All the undiscovered
inventions, sciences, and arts of the future exist in the mind,
but they can come through into expression only in the degree
that an individual opens his consciousness to them. So with
esoteric truth which remains something hidden until it takes
form in consciousness, and then it produces an effect in the
outer world.

As you know the truth, this truth will free you from all
carnal mind conditions, which mean all situations or circumstances conditioned by good or evil. Every bit of truth realized will help to set you free from some phase of good or
evil, until you attain the fullness of the spiritual light in
which Spirit through the instrument of the unconditioned
mind expresses Itself as your being, body, business, home,
and relationships.

But before this can happen there must be a preparation
in which we abide in the Word and let the Word abide in
us, in which we consciously dwell in the Word. After the
experience of illumination, however, life is lived without
effort and without taking thought.

Life is unconditioned: There is no such thing as a new
life or an old life, nor is there a diseased or a healthy life.
Do not try to condition life! Do not try to make it good or
evil! Do not try to have it up or down, longer or shorter, for
there is no such thing. If we do not accept the belief of good
and evil, our life is unconditioned pure spiritual being.

The tempter, the belief of good and evil, stands before us,
as it did before Adam and Eve, only now we understand that
life and mind are unconditioned and we turn on the tempter
as did Jesus: "Get thee behind me, Satan. I accept no conditioning of my life. My mind, life, Soul, and body are unconditioned, unfettered, and free, knowing neither good nor
evil, knowing only God-being, pure Spirit, pure Soul, pure
Life."

# CHAPTER VII

# A ROSE IS A ROSE IS A ROSE

No one can free himself from the belief in two powers and make the return to Eden until he is willing to relinquish his human judgments and look out upon the world with an unconditioned mind. The practice of seeing neither good nor evil can begin at this very moment with any object which comes within range of your vision or with any person with whom you may be confronted. In most cases, however, it is simpler to begin the practice with some object or person with whom you are not emotionally involved.

The practice might begin with a bouquet of flowers which may have been sent to you as a gift. If you have no precon-ceived idea of them, you do not know whether they are going to give you joy in their beauty or an attack of hay fever. Con-template them, look at them; and if you see them as having power for either good or evil, you will be thinking thoughts about them for a long time to come.

Change all that and acknowledge that these flowers, in and of themselves, have no power whatsoever, that they are not good flowers and they are not bad flowers. At this point, you may be willing to admit that they are not evil, but you may still wonder why they are not good. The answer is that they are not good in the sense that good is embodied in them: The good is in the consciousness of the individual who provided the flowers because that good is love. Love is good, love is invisible and spiritual. Love is the substance that sent these flowers to you, perhaps from a great distance; love is that invisible thing of which these flowers are the visible expression.

If you were to call these flowers good, and then in three or four days they faded and were gone, you would have lost your good, but inasmuch as their only value beyond a momentary sense of pleasure lies in the lasting remembrance of the giver—of the love that prompted them, of the devotion, the friendship and gratitude—it makes no real difference what happens to them. When the flowers themselves have faded and are long since gone and forgotten, still the good, the love and the appreciation of which they were the expression, will remain, creating on the invisible plane an immortal and eternal bond between the giver and the recipient.

For this reason, there should never be grief over the loss of anything to which you have attached value, regardless of how much money it may have cost. The value of the object lies in that which is invisible and which prompted its coming into your experience. The real good is always invisible—it can never be seen, heard, touched, tasted, or smelled—and because it is invisible, it is intangible to human sense.

These flowers, then, in front of you are just flowers—beautiful, yes; nice to look at, yes; colorful, yes; fragrant, yes; but who says they are? Who says they are colorful or fragrant? Ask yourself, "Are they beautiful?" Then wait until you begin to perceive, "Why no, no color registers until those vibrations touch my eyes and my mind interprets them, and then I know that the flowers are yellow; but they are not yellow, they are not beautiful, they are not fragrant until my mind translates these vibrations into beauty, color, and perfume."

As you ponder this, you will find that even the form of

the flowers is not beautiful, in and of itself, but is beautiful only because of your interpretation of it; and as you sit there contemplating them, convinced that these flowers are neither beautiful nor ugly, suddenly into that vacuum which you have created will come the awareness of what it is you are looking at, and then you will find that it is much more than a bowl of roses, and you will be led to this conclusion: "Roses, roses, you are nothing: Using the unconditioned mind as an instrument, I* create you in my own image and likeness; I give you your color, form, beauty, and perfume. This I, however, is not the personal sense of "I," which can never do such things, but the I which is God, that part of me which is my true identity, and it is that I which has created these roses in Its image and likeness, and therefore they are not good and they are not bad—they are perfect. Of themselves, they are nothing, but by virtue of the grace of God they are perfect."

Gradually, it will be revealed to you that these flowers are the very form of God Itself, placed here in your room for some miraculous purpose, not just for the purpose of being admired for a day, but as a part of the allness and fullness and completeness of God in Its beauty and essence.

Everything in this world has a spiritual significance, but you will never discover what that significance is by consulting dictionaries or encyclopedias. You will only come into an awareness of the function and spiritual significance of anything as you turn within to that vacuum which you have created by your realization, "This is not what it appears to be, and of my own self, I cannot interpret this appearance. God alone can interpret it correctly. So now, God, what is it?" Then will come the revelation and the unfoldment of its true identity and spiritual significance.

If you are one who is plagued by lack, it is possible that you may find yourself in such a state of confusion, with your mind so beset with a sense of fear that there may not be a sufficiency, that sometimes you find it very hard to quiet

* Wherever "I" appears in italics, the reference is to God.

your mind enough for a peaceful meditation. But there is a way in which you can meditate, even with these disturbing thoughts uppermost in your consciousness, and your mind will settle down into such a peace and tranquility that God will be able to speak to you about supply.

Take out a piece of money—it makes no difference what its denomination is, whether a coin or currency—and put it in front of you. Look at it. If you can see what I see, you will agree that it is as dead as a doornail—inanimate and lifeless.

If you continue looking at this piece of money and proceed with your cogitations, your thought will eventually turn to where this money came from and how it came into your possession. Perhaps somebody gave it to you as an expression of love or gratitude; or if you earned it, it represents somebody's payment to you for service of some kind. Then you may think of the use that will be made of it. As a piece of metal or paper, it has no value to you; but it can be used as a medium of exchange for marketing or purchases of one kind or another. You are now beginning to lose sight of this object as money and are gaining the vision of its function as something useful, loving, and generous. Soon your mind has gone beyond the money itself, and you begin to see why this money belongs to you.

Once you are able to look at money in this light, you will see that far from its supplying you, it is you who supply money with its capacities and power. By that time your mind has gone from the physical realm into the invisible, and peace descends, quiet comes, and a complete stillness in which you can receive an impartation from God in regard to the true interpretation of money.

If you follow this procedure in regard to anything for which you have grave concern or to which you are unduly attached, you will be given the correct interpretation of it and its function in your experience. For example, whereas the acquisition of money is generally considered desirable, the addiction to alcohol is considered evil, and yet the problem of alcoholism can be handled in much the same way as the problem of supply. When a person begins to realize that alcohol has power neither for good nor for evil, he loses all taste for it. This is also true of gluttony or the tobacco habit. True, many people would be willing to go so far as to agree that these have no power for evil, but at the same time, they still think that they have power to give pleasure or satisfaction. As long as a person gives them any power, however, for good or for evil, they hold him in their grasp.

Many alcoholics have been healed through the understanding that there is no power for evil in alcohol, but I have had greater success in dealing with this particular problem by knowing that there is no power for good in alcohol. Several years ago a very interesting case was brought to me by a woman who told me in great tears and self-righteous horror that her husband had reached the place where he refused to work, that she had to support him, and that he lay in bed every day of the week except on her payday when he got up to go out to buy his weekly supply of whisky, using her hard-earned money to pay for it. The entire situation was just a little bit too much for her to take any longer; but she had become interested in spiritual healing and wanted to know what I could do about it spiritually. It was pure inspiration that led me to say:

"Do you know something? It comes to me that your husband is not an alcoholic at all: You are the alcoholic."

"I don't know what you mean."

"Well, you seem to be more afraid of alcohol than your husband is."

She looked at me uncomprehendingly and said:

"Well, perhaps I am. Every day I see what it is doing. My husband doesn't think it is terrible; he likes it."

"There's a difference of opinion there. You really believe that alcohol is bad, don't you?"

"I certainly do."

"And yet the whole basis of our work is that there is neither good nor evil. Now what are we going to do with that? I can put it to you this way: Suppose your husband wanted to use your money to buy ginger ale, would you object?"

"No, I'd gladly go to work, and he could have all the ginger ale he wanted."

"So, ginger ale is good, but alcohol is evil. That is the appearance again, and there we are back with Adam and Eve. Now let's see who is at fault in this, your husband or you. Your husband thinks that alcohol is good and you think it's evil, so you're deadlocked, I guess, and that is where you are going to stay for a while unless you can begin to see what I see and that is that actually ginger ale isn't good, and whisky isn't bad, that there is no power in either one, *if all power is in God*. That's the vision and the way I see it. God is the infinite all-power, and besides God, there is no power for good or evil."

"Where does that leave me? What am I supposed to do?"

"Suppose we agree that for the next week your husband can have all the whisky he wants, because we know that it has no power for good and that it has no power for evil, so we don't care what he does with it. You go right home and tell him that you've made a serious mistake and that you don't think whisky is so terrible after all, and that from now on, he can have all he wants of it."

That seemed to be going a little too far. She was shocked so she went outside and sat in my outer office for a while, but finally she decided that since nothing else had been effective, she would try this as an experiment, and she said to me when she came back into the office:

"Well, I'm not getting anywhere this way; I can't do worse that way, so I'm going to do it; but it's a pretty hard thing to ask me to do."

"Try it and see."

She went home, waiting for the proper moment, and when her husband wanted whisky, she said:

"Oh, yes, sure, here it is."

He looked at her in surprise, but made no comment until a few days later, when he came to her complaining:

"You know there is no use drinking this stuff. They're

making that wartime whisky again, and it has no punch, no effect—there's no power to the stuff." And that's how he was ultimately freed. He couldn't drink it any more because it no longer gave him the satisfaction he had heretofore received from it.

From my observation, I believe that the majority of alcoholics suffer from alcoholism not so much because they think that its indulgence is evil as because they think they are going to derive some good, that is, some pleasure from it. With the realization that alcohol is not good, their taste for it disappears.

Watch this carefully. Do not make the metaphysical mistake of declaring that evil is not power, but believing that good is. Be quick to recognize that there is no power but God. Do not make the mistake of worshiping or fearing any creature, whether the creature is in physical form or in thought form. Do not fear it and do not glorify it. Glorify the Creator of all form, and when you do that, you have neither good power nor evil power: You have only God-power, and for that one brief second you will be right back in the Garden of Eden where there is not a single problem, where there is not a force or power acting upon you negatively or positively: You are just suspended in an atmosphere of peace.

You could throw every worry aside and never again know a sleepless night if you could put this book down in the conviction that there is nothing good or evil *in and of itself*. In that state of consciousness, there would be nothing to worry you or keep you awake, nor would there be anything to rejoice over. It is true that in following this way of life you do forfeit some of the thrills and excitement of human life. This does not mean, however, that you do not continue to enjoy flowers and music and all the beautiful things of this world. The only difference is that you do not become overly elated about them.

You will be more than compensated for this lack of excitement in the lack of concern you will experience, because you have now come to perceive that there are no qualities of good or evil as such in any person or thing, and that unless you invest him or it with these qualities, no such qualities are present. Whatever the appearance, it is merely a form of some sort, nothing but a blank in front of you until you decide in your own mind that this thing is beautiful or ugly, that this person is good or bad, or that your dog is faithful to you but your neighbor's dog is a pest.

Because your mind and mine have become imbued with the ignorance characteristic of human beliefs, stored full of superstition, environmental and educational conditioning, and medical and psychological knowledge, we do not view people or things as they are. We view them as they appear to be, judging from appearances, and thereby suffer the consequences of such judgment.

The way to free our mind of ignorance, superstition, and fear is to go back to Eden where there is no knowledge of good and evil and lose concern whether we are "naked" or clothed, that is, concern whether we are rich or poor at the moment, whether we have human failings or virtues, whether we are happy or unhappy.

Let us begin where we are at this particular moment and let our spiritual unfoldment begin with the understanding that since God is the principle of this universe, it is perfect. A star is a star; a rose is a rose; a dog is a dog is a dog; and a moon is a moon is a moon is a moon; but let us not call them good, and let us not call them bad: Let us call them by their names—star, rose, dog, moon—and we shall find that God will reveal their nature to us and the correct place and function they are to occupy and perform in our experience.

Everything in the universe emanates from God, but man has sought out many inventions. Man has twisted and turned the spiritual realities of God's creation to destructive purposes, until even the glories of the atom have become the horrors of the atom bomb. Man has done that, not God. God has given us the principles which enable us to fly through the air, but man has utilized these principles for instruments of devastation; and as long as the mind is distorted with ideas of good and evil, the blessings of these God-given ideas will become the tombs for millions of men. When there is no trace of good or evil intent in our mind, however, that unconditioned mind becomes an instrument through which these principles pour out in their purity, harmony, and perfection.

In proportion as we keep our mind free of judgments, it functions without concepts, so that when the principles of life come into expression, they come through as they did through Einstein, as pure law. Similarly, when the Spirit comes through the minds of understanding practitioners who sit in the Silence with no judgment—not trying to get rid of a disease, not trying to overcome a sin, and not trying to destroy a fear, but just sitting there in a vacuum of God's grace—the truth comes through in its purity, and the patient says, "I feel better" or "I have had a healing."

What creates and perpetuates humanhood is the pairs of opposites—the belief that flowers are good but that weeds are evil, the belief that robins are good but the bugs on the rosebushes are evil. If, however, we neither gloss over some evil appearance as good, which is merely an old metaphysical cliché, nor judge it bad, but recognize that all that exists is pure Soul, infinitely expressing Itself, eventually even the bugs on the rosebushes find their rightful place where they cannot perform any destructive function. Even the so-called evil people of the world begin to serve a good purpose—they do, or they are removed from positions where they can work their purposes.

We are approaching a period in the world in which evil will find no room for expression in people, thoughts, and things. It will be crowded right off the earth, because the earth will be so full of the knowledge of this principle of one power that evil will have no channel through which to function. It will be lopped off as fast as it shows its head by this invisible spiritual power that permeates consciousness.

# CHAPTER VIII

# HENCEFORTH KNOW WE NO MAN
## AFTER THE FLESH

The question may arise in your mind, "How can I stop thinking about and believing in good and evil?" Let me give you an example which may help to clarify this point. Look at your hand, and ask yourself, "Is it a good hand or is it a bad hand?" And if you carry out into practice what you have learned thus far, you will have to admit that your hand is neither good nor bad: It is just a hand, a piece of flesh and a bundle of bones. It has no power to act *in* or *of itself*: It cannot pet and it cannot punch; it cannot give and it cannot withhold. But you can move it; you can use it as an instrument for giving or withholding. You can do such things, but the *hand* cannot.

The hand is but an instrument for your use. It can be used for various purposes: It can give generously and benevolently or steal unashamedly, but this hand cannot of itself do anything. There has to be something to move the hand. Since you govern your hand, you can empower it to do good or evil, and not only can you empower the hand but also the body, sometimes to do good and sometimes to do evil.

However, when you have transcended mind and thought, it is then that both mind and body are governed and controlled by the *I* that is God, and this produces a mind, body, and daily experience which are neither good nor evil but spiritual. The secret again is in the attainment of the unconditioned mind through which the Soul functions as life and experience.

The very moment you are willing to admit that this hand can of its own self do nothing, it is governed by the *I*, and from then on it becomes an instrument of God carrying with it only the power to bless, because you and I, of our own human selves, are no longer governing this hand: Now *I* am, and *I* is God.

Turn now from consideration of your hand and take your whole body into your mind and realize this same truth: You do not have a good or a bad body, a young or an old body. Your body is merely so much flesh and bones. In and of itself, it has no intelligence; it knows nothing about either disease or health; it knows nothing about time—nothing about calendars. Unfortunately, the human "I" does, and because of that, the body changes. The body knows nothing about seasons of the year, whether it is winter or summer, good weather or bad, but again, unfortunately, we do, and because of that the body reflects whatever we accept in our mind.

It is the mind which becomes the avenue through which the body takes on the beliefs of the world. It is the mind, then, which determines whether the body is good or bad, young or old, well or sick, but when there is neither a good body nor a bad one, a young one nor an old one, from that moment on, *I*, which is the presence and power of God, takes over and begins to manifest Its conditions on the body.

When we begin to realize that our body is the temple of the living God, we place our body at God's disposal to use as He chooses, and then our body becomes an instrument for God, for the *I* at the center of our being. But we have to be willing to make some sort of a beginning, and that is done by knowing that there is no good or evil in body—that body as such has no qualities of its own: It merely expresses that which is imposed upon it.

This reversal or change of attitude toward body and the conditions imposed upon it is begun by consciously realizing:

*There is no good or evil in my body: There is no age or youth in it; there is no strength or weakness in it. My body is just an instrument for the I, the God within me, which is the creative and maintaining Principle of my being.*

Think for a few moments on the vital problems that are disturbing you—your own, your children's, or your grandchildren's. As you think about them, ask yourself, "Are these conditions good or evil? Who said so? Who decreed that they are good or evil?" Then ask yourself, "Did God create evil?" I think you know better than to answer that in the affirmative.

If God created eternality and immortality, if there is nothing in Him "that defileth or maketh a lie," certainly He did not create evil. But, if God did not create evil, who did? Did anyone, or have you been entertaining a *belief* in good and evil? Who gave you that belief? Where did such a belief come from? You may not know the answer to that question now, but as you work with the principle which is the theme of this book, the answer to this, as well as many other questions, will be revealed to you. At this time, however, why not be willing to accept the premise that in reality there is neither good nor evil?

When you reach the point where you can understand that all human conditions of whatever name or nature exist but as a belief in the human mind, a belief that resulted in man's expulsion from the Garden of Eden, and when you become convinced in your innermost heart that because God is infinite there are no pairs of opposites, you can say with the Master, "I have overcome the world." Then, you are back in the kingdom of heaven where nobody knows what health is because nobody knows what disease is; nobody knows what painlessness is because nobody knows what pain is; nobody knows what wealth is because nobody knows what poverty is; and if one does not know what health and wealth are, how can one know what their opposites are? There is nothing with which to make comparisons: There is just God, just spiritual Being, perfection.

As we approach the healing work, we should have in our consciousness no awareness of evil to be removed or risen above, but because so much of humanhood remains in most of us, we still recognize that there is before us the appearance of evil in the form of sin, disease, death, lack, and limitation, and as long as we are faced with such appearances, we cannot be absolute and, ostrich-like, ignore the appearance, repeating over and over again, "Oh, God is all; there is no error." That is useless and foolish. We should not do that; we should let God say it to us; and when we hear the still small Voice or when we feel that stirring within us, we may be assured that whatever appearance of sin, disease, death, lack, or limitation is before us will melt away. But do not think that you humanly can ever be so wise as to bring this about.

Because you know the words and can say orally or silently, "There is neither good nor evil," do not believe that their repetition will work miracles in your life, because it will not. You have to live with this truth until you can demonstrate it; you have to prove it over and over again within yourself. Moreover, never forget that if you are tempted to tell this to any man before it becomes so evident that the world sees it in you, you will lose what you have received and, what is more, you may lose even the possibility of demonstrating it in this incarnation, because no one can trifle with the word of God, no one can boast with it and play with it, and think that he can retain it.

You can only prove this principle in the degree that you hug it tightly within yourself—keep it sacred and keep it secret—but use it. Use it morning, noon, and night with every bit of error that confronts you, whether in the newspaper, on the radio, in your family, or on the street. Wherever and whenever you are faced with error, turn and ask yourself, "Can this make me believe in good or evil? Can I be made to accept two powers?" If you can do that, you will refrain from accepting or judging by appearances and you will not be tempted to try to heal somebody or something, but you will stay within yourself and judge righteous judgment, stay within the Garden of Eden which represents your spiritual domain, the state of divine harmony.

Righteous judgment knows, "In the beginning God. God created all that was made; God looked at what He had made and found it very good." Are you able to hold to that truth? As ugly appearances stick up their heads, are you able to overcome the temptation to be fooled by them? Are you able to declare and know within yourself, "I accept God alone as constituting the very substance of all life. I cannot be made to accept either good or evil because there is only Spirit; there is only one life."

Spiritual healing cannot take place on the human plane. It can take place only when you have stopped thinking of the person and the disease and the condition and the belief and the claim and have returned to Eden where there is only God, Spirit—wholeness and completeness. Nobody can ever be a spiritual healer who works from the standpoint of effect or who prays from the standpoint of trying to correct something in the Adam-world because, if he succeeded, he would but have exchanged an unpleasant dream for a pleasant one. If he succeeded in improving the human picture, he would only have good materiality instead of bad materiality. He would be no nearer the kingdom of God.

At one time I was sitting in a room with a person who was to all sense very near death, and I felt the same discomfort that anyone would feel in similar circumstances because I realized that there was nothing I could do to prevent his passing. I had no miraculous gifts or any miracle-working words that would prevent the apparently inevitable. Something had to come to me from the depths of the within, or there was going to be a funeral. All I could do was to turn within to that still small Voice and wait and wait and wait, and sometimes beg and plead.

Finally it came, and these were the words, "This is my beloved Son, in whom I am well pleased!" No one would have believed that if he had seen him. Here was disease in its final form; here was a person dying, and yet despite the appearance the Voice said, "This is my beloved Son, in whom I am well pleased." After those words came, it was not long before they became an actual fact in demonstration; and health, harmony, and completeness were restored.

On another occasion, I was called to my own father's side when he lay in an oxygen tent and, according to the physicians in attendance, was on his deathbed. I stood there with no words of wisdom that could change this appearance into health; I stood there just as anyone would stand in front of his own father in such a situation—but with this difference: I knew that if God uttered His voice, the earth would melt. Standing there, watching my father breathing through that apparatus, the words came, "Man does not live by breath alone." In less than five minutes, he signaled for the nurse to take the instrument away, and two days later he was out of the hospital.

Who decreed that that condition was evil? God did not; God merely said, "Man shall not live by breath alone," thus dissipating the belief that man lives by breath, and proving that he lives by the word of God.

Only as long as you entertain the belief in two powers, can you be in difficulty. You are free as soon as you begin to look upon all conditions with a "Who told you, you are naked? Who told you, you are evil? Who told you this is sin? Who told you this is disease? Who told you this is dangerous? Where did it come from? Did God ever say that to anyone?"

The very moment that you perceive that your function as

a spiritual healer is not to remove or heal disease or believe that God heals disease or that there are some formulas or affirmations that will remove disease, but that your function is to know the truth that this whole mortal creation is made up of the belief in good and evil, you will know neither health nor disease, poverty nor wealth, but only a continuous outpouring of spiritual harmony—the Garden of Eden.

You never will be a spiritual healer as long as you believe there are two powers—the power of God and the power of sin, disease, lack, or power in astrology or diets. You never will be a spiritual healer until you know that you do not need any power. God is maintaining His spiritual universe eternally, and there is nothing wrong with it. What is wrong is with us; what is wrong is this universal belief in two powers.

In the second chapter of Genesis, God is no longer the creator, but now there is a being called Lord God; and Lord, it is said, is synonymous with law. In other words, the man of the second chapter of Genesis lives under the law, whereas the man of the first chapter, created in the image and likeness of God, lives under Grace.

How can we become that man who lives under Grace? How else except by giving up the belief in two powers? Then Grace permeates our entire being; Grace supports, maintains, and sustains us; and Grace goes before us to make the crooked places straight. Grace is all about us, and yet we have no more awareness of it than a fish has of water. The fish is swimming in the water, but it does not know it. A bird knows nothing about air: It is flying through it, but flying unthinkingly. In the words of Francis Thompson:

> Does the fish soar to find the ocean,
> The eagle plunge to find the air—
> That we ask of the stars in motion
> If they have rumor of thee there?

And so it is that when we are in a state of spiritual health, we not only do not know disease, but we do not know health —we only know that we are harmonious, normal, and free.

How can a healthy man describe health? It is impossible because he does not know it: He only knows that he is in it, whatever it may be, and it is nice to be.

Let us understand that somewhere, sometime, somehow, we have accepted a belief that is no part of us, a belief that there are two powers—a God-power that can do something for us and is not doing it, and a power of evil that is very much in operation. God-power is already doing all that it can do, and it is operating in the Edenic state of consciousness for all spiritual creation, but it cannot operate in the world of two powers.

That is the reason that as good, moral, and benevolent as we or our neighbors may be, we and they come under sin, death, accident, and wars. But over and over again the question is asked, "How can such things be if there is a God?" And the answer is a startling one: There is a God, but there is *no God in the human scene*; there is no God in the second chapter of Genesis: There is only a Lord God which is the law of cause and effect—karmic law. When we rise above the law of cause and effect, we are no longer under the law, but under Grace, or in other words we are living in the first chapter of Genesis where no such thing as human good or human evil exists. There is no sin, and there is no purity: There is just God.

If we have a problem, either our own or a problem of some member of our family, of a friend, patient, or student, or if somebody is looking to us for harmony because of our greater understanding, this principle of neither good nor evil must be practiced in our meditation:

*Father, here I am waiting to commune with You, but for what purpose? Is it to turn evil into good? If that is what is necessary here, would You not have done that before I had an opportunity to ask You to do it? But yet You do not seem to be doing anything about it, so perhaps that is not the need.*

*"Where the Spirit of the Lord is, there is liberty"—where*

the Spirit of the Lord is, there is no evil. Then what becomes of the evil? Nobody has ever discovered where darkness goes when the light is let in, but when the sun comes up there is light, and in the presence of the sun, there is no darkness. In the presence of God, there is no sin, no false appetite, no disease, lack, or unemployment, no insecurity or danger, because all such things evaporate in His presence.

Where God is, I find no evil: I find God—God as my high tower, God as the health of my countenance, God as my supply, God as my all in all.

Whatever this is, in and of itself, it is neither good nor evil, because there is no good or evil anywhere present; there is only God, filling all space; so there is nothing to be made good, and there is nothing that can lapse from good. God formed this universe out of Himself; therefore, it is God that is good, not the condition or the thing; and even though appearances may testify to either good or evil, I do not accept them.

God constitutes my body, which is the temple of God. God is my dwelling place; God is the health of my countenance; God is the secret place of the most High in which I live and move and have my being.

To heal, it is necessary to transcend thought. Even though a meditation begins as a contemplation of truth, it must, before the healing is accomplished, rise into the higher realm of silent awareness. At the beginning of a healing meditation a passage of truth, such as "Henceforth know we no man after the flesh," may come into thought. After that has repeated itself several times, or after we have consciously repeated it, thought slows down as we ponder the meaning of knowing no man after the flesh: Henceforth know we no man after good flesh or bad flesh; henceforth know we no man as sick or well, rich or poor; henceforth know we only God appearing as individual spiritual man.

This is the secret of The Infinite Way, and it is the secret of healing: "Henceforth know we no man after the flesh"—

not even after healthy flesh. Henceforth know we no man after his wealth—large amounts or small: We know only God as Father, and God as Son, the Christ, the spiritual image and likeness of God. Henceforth know we only God as constituting man; henceforth know we only God as the substance of man. Henceforth know we only God as the life of man, the Soul of man, the health of man, the wealth of man, the dwelling place of man. Henceforth know we only God, and not man.

Now we perceive that man is not flesh, but consciousness, possessing only spiritual qualities. We discern that there is a creative Principle which produces Its own image and likeness, and that this creative Principle is also the sustaining Principle of life, and therefore Its creation must necessarily be of Its own essence—Life, Love, Spirit, Soul. This is the true nature of man.

"Henceforth know we no man after the flesh." Then how do we know him? As the son of God, his true identity. As we know ourselves and everyone else to be spiritual offspring, we never look at the body, but look right through the eyes until we can see way back of them beyond mortal man, see beyond young man or old man, sick man or well man, to where the Christ sits enthroned. Visible man, whether sick or well, is not the Christ-man. It is the spiritual Self that is that man, and that Christ-man is not subject to the laws of the flesh, not even harmonious flesh, but is subject only to the Christ.

Soon one reaches the end of such mental cogitation or contemplation and settles into a quiet, peaceful state of receptivity into which no thought intrudes. In that state of consciousness, the healing Christ takes over, flooding consciousness with tranquility and peace. It is a spiritual "peace, be still," and from this emanates the healing Grace which envelops one or one's patient, and then harmony becomes apparent and tangible in experience.

In our meditation, we may sit down with a sick person in our mind, or with a poor or sinful one, but we should not get up until, through realization, we have come to that place where there is no man, sick or well, rich or poor, sinful or pure; there is no sick person to be made well and no well person over whom to rejoice: *There is only God—there is only God appearing as the Father and God appearing as the Son.* Then is our prayer complete and with it comes the conviction, "It is so."

As long as we are knowing the truth—thinking, declaring, or voicing truth—we are in the mental realm. True, we may be thinking of spiritual things, but we are thinking of spiritual things mentally, and no healing is likely to take place. If healing does occur in some such cases, it is through mental argument, and it is not spiritual but mental healing, the effect of suggestion, the fruitage of the type of practice which says, "You are well" or "You are perfect" or "God's will is done in you"; and the mind accepts the suggestion and responds to it. That is not spiritual healing because the patient has merely responded to the suggestion of another mind.

In The Infinite Way, we do not make suggestions; we never use the word you in a treatment; we never use the name of the patient nor do we take the name of the disease, complaint, or condition into the treatment, nor do we let the person enter our thought after he has asked for help. Even though we are still in the mental realm when we contemplate, it is not about the patient: It is about God and the things of God that we know, or the laws of God that we understand or have read about and are now trying to realize.

We do not expect healing from any of this because we cannot bring forth the son of God from the second chapter of Genesis, out of which comes only Adam, the man of flesh. The only way that this man of flesh can be restored to Eden and to his normal spiritual harmony is not by thinking thoughts about him, but by entering into a state of Silence which recognizes neither good nor evil.

When we have no desires, we have no desire for good any more than we have a desire for evil, and then we are pure enough to be in the Garden of Eden which is desireless. It is not a state of desiring good, but a contentedness with being.

# CHAPTER IX

# THIS IS A SPIRITUAL UNIVERSE

Several years ago when I was on my way to South Africa, I stopped off for a day in the Belgian Congo, and after the man in charge of the bookings and his assistant had taken care of all my tickets, made whatever examinations were necessary, and weighed my luggage, I called a little native boy to carry my three bags out to the plane which I was boarding for Johannesburg. This was such a small air station that I could see the boy as he walked out of the gate onto the field with one large piece of baggage in each hand and a small piece under his arm. A few minutes later he returned without any baggage and I said to him questioningly, "O.K.?" to which he replied, "O.K."

When I arrived in Johannesburg the next morning, there was only the one tiny little piece of baggage waiting for me, and the other two large pieces were missing. Immediately, the personnel of this tremendously big and active airport at Johannesburg began searching for my baggage, but they did not find it in the enclosure nor was it with the crew's baggage; and furthermore when they sent someone to search the plane, there was no baggage there, either. The person in charge of the airline said that he would immediately contact the station in the Belgian Congo and would soon have an answer for me, so there was nothing for me to do but go to my hotel.

The Infinite Way students in Johannesburg had arranged for me to visit Krueger National Park, so after buying some necessary clothing, we started out on our three-day trek through this fabulous wild-animal preserve with the full expectation of picking up my baggage when we returned. But upon our return no baggage had as yet been found. The only explanation the airline had to offer was that somebody must have stolen it, and that that somebody must have been the little native boy and a confederate because the last time the bags were seen was when he had picked them up and carried them out onto the field. The absurdity of such an assumption should have been apparent at once because certainly nobody could have taken those two heavy pieces of luggage away from the airfield without being noticed. Nevertheless, all the native quarters in the town were searched, and the place turned upside down because the authorities were convinced that a theft had occurred. Despite all this hullabaloo, however, no baggage was found.

For three weeks, I was in South Africa without baggage and without money—without purse and without scrip—but this was no great hardship because I ate regularly, my hotel bills were paid, and clothing was purchased, although only the absolute necessities, because I was convinced that my bags would show up, which was a very wrong conviction.

Two nights before I was to leave for India, I sat down to give this whole incident some serious consideration. "This represents a failure on my part. What is that failure? What has gone wrong here?"

As I sat in my room, pondering and meditating, finally the answer came: "This is a spiritual universe, and yet here I am waiting for baggage, when the truth of the matter is there isn't any baggage. All that baggage is, is part of the belief of time and space—space that is occupied by baggage, time in which it could be lost, and space in which it could be lost. Here we are trying to find baggage, which if it were found would only be an evidence that the human scene had been manipulated.

"There is no truth to this whole picture because we are living in a spiritual universe where nobody has any need of baggage. Whatever there is of reality is incorporeal, spiritual, and omnipresent; and whatever appears as finite baggage in time and space must be an image in thought, and it can have no reality to it; so I have been fooled into hoping and waiting for material baggage to turn up in a spiritual universe where every idea is omnipresent."

With that I retired.

The story came to a quick conclusion after that realization. The assistant manager of the airline at the station in Johannesburg was seated at his desk at eight o'clock the next morning when, apparently out of nothing, the thought came to him, "Baggage can't dissolve into thin air. It just couldn't disappear between here and there—it has to be somewhere. Just where is it?" Suddenly another idea struck him, and he went to the hotel where the crew was lodged on overnight stops, and there were the two pieces of baggage on the floor where they had been waiting for three weeks. Nobody had thought of that possibility; in fact, nobody thought of any kind of a practical solution until I *stopped thinking about baggage*.

This story illustrates a very important point in spiritual living and healing. Ordinarily, in metaphysics we would think, "Oh, well, it has to turn up" or "It can't be lost." In other words, we would be dealing with an *it*—an *it* called baggage. The fallacy of this method of meeting a problem is immediately apparent because in the case of illness, in order to be consistent, we would have to give a treatment that dealt specifically with heart, liver, lungs, stomach, digestion, elimination, head, or foot, and we would be completely outside the realm of spiritual being. Most of us do know enough not to treat people by name and we know enough not to treat hearts, livers, and lungs; but just see how easily we can be fooled into looking for baggage.

We become very sure of ourselves and believe that we are going along in the right direction, and then all of a sudden the hypnotism of human sense can make us think about baggage or the lack of it. Now please understand that I was not concerned about the loss of the baggage: My mistake was that I was sure it would turn up, which is exactly like being sure that a person's heart is going to get well, or that his sick foot is going to be better; whereas the principle upon which all our work is based is that of the real creation as recounted in the first chapter of Genesis in which God made all that was made, and all that He made is good.

The spiritual creation is an incorporeal creation, and the proof of that is that there was light before there was a sun in the sky. If we live and move and have our being in the spiritual creation as set forth in the first chapter of Genesis, we can have everything we need without having baggage. The sense-world, that which we can see, hear, taste, touch, and smell, is the unreal creation described in the second chapter of Genesis—a mental image in mind. If we remember that, we shall not try to manipulate the human scene or handle the mental image which exists only as a shadow within our thought, and then we shall be witnesses to the quick dissolution of these mental images.

Do not mistake or misunderstand what I am saying: I know that when we are traveling baggage seems real and necessary. I also know that most of the time our concept of body seems real because one thing or another brings it into our awareness, and because of that, there is the temptation to think of it as real. We do not deny the body. It is real, but what we see as body is not body: It is a mental image within our own thought—a universal mental concept, individualized within us.

There is no such thing as a material body: There is only a material concept of body. There is no such thing as a material universe: There are only material concepts of the one spiritual universe. As long as we accept a material concept of universe, we are under the laws of matter, but we are free as soon as we begin to understand that we live and move and have our being in the first chapter of Genesis where man is made in the image and likeness of God, or Spirit, and that the Soul of God is the Soul of man, the life of God is the life of man, the mind of God is the mind of man, the body of God is the body of man.

"Know ye not that your body is the temple of the Holy Ghost"—not the body as it is seen in the mirror, but as it actually is. Just as my realization that we were not dealing with material baggage, but with Omnipresence, immediately awakened the one man necessary to the demonstration—awakened him to the idea of Omnipresence—and right where he was, was where he found the baggage, so in times of problems, to understand what body is and what this universe is, is to arrive at a realization that would bring the solution:

*I live and move and have my being in God; I am in my Father, and my Father is in me. How can I be finite or limited if an infinite Father is within me? How can a finite, limited being have an infinite God within Him? Therefore, I must be as spiritual as the Father that created me.*

*All being must be spiritual, and into this spiritual creation, nothing finite can enter to limit or create any sense of separation.*

The suffering of this world is due to our looking around for a piece of material baggage—even expecting it to be in its right place. That is the error. There is no place for you or me or for any "he," "she," or "it," except in the only place where it is to be found and that is in Omnipresence, where even that which to human sense seems absent is present.

On a cloudy day, the sun seems to be absent when it is merely hidden from our view. Just so, the clouds of human belief and the density of human thought may temporarily hide from us that which is omnipresent, that which is present where *I* am. And what is it that is present where *I am?* All that the Father has is omnipresent—integrity, loyalty, fidelity, eternality, immortality, justice, freedom, joy, harmony of every name and nature—unless we *finitize* it and see it as a piece of baggage, something that occupies time and space.

Nothing occupies time or space but our mental images, and the reason they do is because we accept a yesterday, a today, and a tomorrow. The minute we rise above the mental realm of life, we shall perceive that there is no such thing as time. Anyone who has ever made a God-contact has discovered that he had no awareness of time while he was in that experience, because even though the contact may have lasted only half a minute, enough took place in that half minute to convince him that several hours must have gone by. Other times when the contact is made, it may seem that something like a minute must have gone by, and then when we look at our watch we find that two or three hours have elapsed.

In other words, there is no such thing as an awareness of either time or space in the consciousness of Omnipresence. We are in the mental state of consciousness when we are thinking and reasoning, or when we are beholding anything as person or thing. It is only in the spiritual realm that we transcend mind.

People have sought for a way to transcend mind through a process which has been described as stilling the mind, and they have found that such attempts frequently result, not in achieving spiritual consciousness, but in quite the opposite effect, a dulling of consciousness. There is a way, however, in which we can rise above the mental level of life, although we may not be able to remain there permanently because to do that requires years and years of devotion to this and to nothing else; but we can rise above mind to such a degree that, at least when we are in the world, it will no longer disturb us to any great extent.

A beginning can be made by not attempting to stop our thinking processes. If the mind wants to think, we let it, and if necessary, even sit and watch it as it goes through the thinking process. No matter what thoughts come, they can do us no harm. They have no power, and there is nothing in them for us to fear. If we fear or hate them, we may try to stop them, and on the other hand if we love them, we may try to hold on to them. So let us not hate or fear any thought that comes to our mind, but also let us not love or try to hold on to any thought regardless of how good it may seem to be.

We let the thoughts come and go while we sit and watch as beholders. All we are looking at are shadows that flit across the screen: There is no power in them, nor any substance; there is no law in them, nor any cause—they are just shadows. Some of them may be very sweet, and we may want to cling to them. Some may disturb or frighten us, but they are only thoughts—thoughts and nothing else. They may testify to disease; they may testify to sin, or they may testify to accident, but no matter how frightening they are, we sit unmoved and watch them come and go:

*There is neither good nor evil in what I am beholding: These things are merely pictures, without power. They cannot do anything; they cannot testify to anything; and even if they seem to be good, they are not good because they are only pictures.*

If we try this little experiment in our meditation periods, we soon will see that we have suffered because these pictures and thoughts have so flooded us and we have become so frightened that we have tried to run away from them or blot them out; and yet, when we are able to see them in their correct perspective, they are inoffensive nothingness, just shadows.

True, sometimes they represent man-made theories or man-made rules with man-made punishment attached to them. But does that endow them with authority? So let us look at them: This one testifies to infection and contagion, and that one to false appetites. The next one is a prophecy of disaster, another one is a fear of lack, and still another is a fear of fear; but the truth is that these are only names, terrible names certainly because of their tragic connotation, but nevertheless only names—names that Adam gave to something which he did not understand—only images in thought.

Let us stop being afraid of names. Even if it is a picture on an x-ray machine, why should we be afraid of it? It is still only a picture, a picture of mind's image. When we no longer have it in mind, it is no longer possible to have a picture of it. We can only take in pictures of that which is being held in mind. If we can see it, hear it, taste it, touch it, or smell it, it is an activity of mind, a mental image, the "arm of flesh"—nothingness. It is a false creation which God never made.

All the time that we are thinking this, we are still in the mental realm, the realm of knowing the truth; but as we continue this exercise, looking squarely at the picture, we begin to realize that it is a picture without substance or cause. Regardless of how material the condition appears to be, it is not any more material than was my lost baggage, and that was not material: It was a mental image, the realization of which revealed Omnipresence.

Sometimes in following such a practice, people are likely to see beautiful pictures or visions, and then they make the mistake, first of all, of trying to hold on to them, and then they make a second mistake of wanting to bring them back at some future time. This is very unwise. We should never do that, never hold on to even a beautiful image, because it is only an image. If it is of God, God can give us as many more as we need, and if it is an unpleasant picture, we must learn not to be afraid of it because it has no existence as externalized reality, but only as a mental image.

Eventually, we come to a place where there is nothing more to be said or thought, so we have only one last word for it:

*Regardless of what you seem to be or claim to be, there are no properties of good or evil inherent in you. All properties are in the Consciousness that made this universe in Its own image and likeness, and neither good nor evil is in form or effect.*

*Whatever your name or nature, if you exist in time or space, you are a mental image, a nothingness. I do not have to fear you because you have no existence in my or anyone's being. You have existence only in mind, and as a mind-existence, you are without form and void. You have no more good or evil in you than the picture on the moving-picture screen —you are just a substanceless shadow.*

When we achieve complete quietness and peace, the mind is no longer functioning, and we have transcended mind and risen into the atmosphere of Spirit, in which we are receptive and responsive to whatever God imparts. As soon as we become unattached, that is, as soon as we are detached from thought—from hate, fear, or love of objects or people so that they can float in front of our eyes with the utmost indifference to us—we are no longer in the realm of mind: We are then reaching, touching, or being touched by our own Soul, which is God, and we are in an atmosphere where, when God speaks, we can hear Him. When God utters His voice, the earth melts, and all problems dissolve.

## PART THREE

# FROM LAW TO GRACE

# CHAPTER X

# YE HAVE HEARD IT SAID OF OLD

At any moment of our experience—it makes no difference whether we are nine, nineteen, or ninety—we can begin the return to the Father's house. But let us not believe that we can return to that Edenic state by continuing to be the same persons we were yesterday with all our human virtues and failings, vacillating constantly between good and evil. Our human virtues will not gain us entry into Eden any more than will our human failings. We have to lose both human failings and human virtues and take on the mantle of the Christ by rising above the mental creation of the second chapter of Genesis which has chained us to the law of good and evil.

"The law was given by Moses, but grace and truth came by Christ Jesus." For hundreds of years before Moses, the Hebrews had been living in a state of slavery with little or no opportunity to make advances in education, culture, religion, art, or the sciences; and under such circumstances it is not surprising that they were living without any greatly developed moral sense. To these people, Moses presented a higher way of life, the backbone of which was the Ten Commandments. If those commandments were obeyed, a person was considered as fine a type of citizen as could be expected, and moreover, if in addition to that he also obeyed the dietetic laws and a few other customs, he merited the title of a good Hebrew. If the law were disobeyed, all the offender could expect was to be stoned or excommunicated. Little or no concept of love was embraced in this teaching. It was strictly a teaching of moral and ethical laws.

A moral or ethical sense, high as it may be, however, is only a step on the way to spiritual consciousness. While a person may live in absolute obedience to the Ten Commandments he may still be eons away from the spiritual life because the true spiritual life is a living above the pairs of opposites.

When Jesus came, he taught a way of life which was not primarily concerned with changing the negative sense of life into the positive, but with rising above *both* the negative and the positive into the spiritual. It should not be forgotten that as a Hebrew rabbi in the organized Hebrew church, Jesus was authorized to speak and preach from its platform; nor should it be forgotten that what he preached was not called Christianity: There was no Christianity. Moreover, he did not preach to Christians: There were no Christians. He was a Hebrew rabbi preaching to Hebrews.

But now a miracle takes place. This man Jesus received an illumination which gave him an entirely new religious teaching, something which heretofore had been unknown to the Hebrews. Now he goes far beyond the karmic law of the Old Testament in his teaching of one power. As he taught this revelation to the men and women of his day, it made them free of all ritual and dogma, so free that the church would not tolerate the man or his teaching. What else but hatred and fear could they feel for one of their own who turned his back upon some of their long established and most cherished practices, such as the insistence on a pilgrimage to Jerusalem once a year for the purpose of paying tithes as well as the observance of other rituals. Jesus' very turning away from these observances was a silent criticism and condemnation of that in which they had placed their trust for so long.

Jesus brought to light the truth that spiritual welfare is in no way related to the rigid observance of any forms, but has to do with the state of consciousness developed by the individual. He preached a new dimension of life, a higher consciousness, which required a *dying* to old beliefs. He made it clear that new wine cannot be added to old bottles, that is, that this new dispensation could not merely be added to the old Hebraic mode of life, but that the old would have to be exchanged for the new because the two were contradictory.

In the Sermon on the Mount, Jesus summarizes the difference between Judaism and his new teaching which was not yet known as Christianity but as the teaching of a radical and independent-thinking Hebrew rabbi. And what is the teaching of this man who was undoubtedly the most illumined and spiritually developed of anyone ever known, so illumined that today the world practically revolves around his teachings?

The word Grace will reveal what it is. The law came by Moses, "but grace and truth by Jesus Christ." This grace and truth mean something quite different from what is meant by the law. And so for three hundred years after Jesus' ministry, there were people traveling up and down the Holy Land, crossing over into Rome and Greece, teaching and preaching not the law as set forth in the Hebrew faith, but a something new, a something startling, something different called grace and truth which gradually came to be known as the teaching of Christianity.

The first followers of his teaching were called Jewish Christians because they were Jews who were followers of the Christ. In fact, in those early days, only those who were Hebrews could become Christians. But eventually Paul and Peter realized that this Christ-teaching was more than just a different kind of Judaism. It was unique, something separate and distinct of its own, and gradually it came to pass that in order to become a Christian, it was not necessary to be a

Hebrew first: Circumcision was no longer required, and many other time-honored practices were forsaken; the disciples began to preach to the Gentiles and to acknowledge that this teaching of the Christ was universal in its nature, until the day came when even the pagans of Rome and Greece or any man, regardless of his background, could, if he would, become a Christian.

So for several hundred years this was the state of the Christian teaching, and then one of the strangest events that has ever happened in the history of the world took place. A church was organized that adopted all the rites and rituals of the Egyptians and other pagans of the day, that accepted bodily and literally Judaism as taught in the Old Testament, discarded all the Christian teaching except the name of its revelator, and then called itself the Christian church. But what happened to this Christ-teaching when it became thus organized? Did this church practice Jesus' teaching of "resist not evil," or did it still cling to the ye-have-heard-it-said-of-old teaching of an "eye for an eye, and a tooth for a tooth"?

The practice of true Christianity lifts the Adamic man who would wreak vengeance on his enemy from the karmic law state of consciousness to the consciousness of grace and truth which reveals a God of love instead of a God of rewards and punishments.

The God Jesus revealed was of an entirely different nature from that of the Old Testament, and in that part of the Sermon on the Mount which deals with karmic law, Jesus taught that sin is punished by the sin itself, but no reference is made to a God who punishes. It is clearly explained that as we do unto others, it will be done unto us—not by God, but according to the karmic law of *as ye sow, so shall ye reap* under which all human beings live. Our deeds of love are reflected back to us in love, and our evil deeds are brought back to us in evil effects by the very act itself. By our own state of consciousness, we set in motion both the good and the evil. "With what measure ye mete, it shall be measured to you again"—not by God, but by the law.

When we hate, we are invoking the law, and when we love, we are invoking the law; when we give or share, we are invoking the law, just as we are when we hold on to things. On every hand, nature testifies to the truth of this law. For example, unless the fruit on the tree is plucked or in some way removed from the tree, the tree will stop bearing. We do not blame God for that—God is not punishing the tree. It is a law of nature that the tree must yield up its fruit in order that it may bring forth more fruit. So unless we yield up, surrender, or release good, we become barren because the law is: "Whatsoever a man soweth, that shall he also reap."

This law of sowing and reaping is applicable to individuals as well as to nations. There is no way to avoid the penalty of wrongdoing—not that there is any God who is going to do anything about it, but because there is a karmic law that each person sets in operation by his actions.

All this the Master revealed in that part of his teaching in the Sermon on the Mount in which he said, "Ye have heard that it hath been said. . . ." But the Master never taught that God punishes—no, not even the thief on the cross, not the woman taken in adultery, not the man born blind. Always it was, "Go, and sin no more." What evil we are experiencing we are bringing upon ourselves—it is not God inflicting it on us.

When Christianity became organized, it adopted the Old Testament teaching of a punishing God, perhaps in the vain hope that it might frighten people into being good; but as a matter of fact that very teaching, far from being a deterrent to evil-doing, is probably responsible for many of the sins committed in the world today. Evil-doers soon discover that there is no God who does anything to them, and the evidence they see about them does not convince them that God will punish either their evils of omission or commission.

If men were taught that the *evil deed itself* punished them, they would understand Jesus' interpretation of karmic law, and then they would be prepared to accept his higher teaching of how to overcome that law. It is possible to set aside karmic law, wipe out all punishment for our former misdeeds and live under Grace, but this cannot happen to anyone individually or to the world until the karmic law as explained by the Master is first learned and understood.

The deed itself carries with it its own reward and its own punishment. It does not have to be an overt act, because the act itself is only the outward expression of the thought impelling the act. Therefore, for example, it is not necessary to steal to bring down the punishment of karmic law: It is only necessary to think of stealing, and actually it is not even necessary to think about it. Merely desiring what somebody else has is sufficient to set in motion karmic law. It is not necessary to strike a person—to become angry with him is enough to bring the law down upon us.

People in grosser states of consciousness do not feel the repercussions of karmic law as quickly as those on the spiritual path who suffer more as a result of a minor infraction of the law than others from a major one, because they have a greater awareness of what is right and what is wrong, and the slightest deviation from the way sets the law in operation.

Setting aside karmic law involves first of all a recognition that it exists—that the evil that we think or do reacts upon us—and then this realization prevents us from blaming somebody or some set of circumstances or conditions for any predicament in which we may find ourselves. We begin to see that we alone are responsible. There is not a mysterious God somewhere chalking up our errors against us, but we, ourselves, determine the issues of life by understanding that we have set in motion the good and the evil that befall us. That leads us to stop blaming or condemning other people and makes us realize that some change must take place within us and that the state of consciousness which made it possible for us to do wrong, either carelessly, thoughtlessly, or sometimes willfully, must be transformed.

Very quickly we learn what Paul discovered—that there are two of us. Each one of us is a dual person, one the creature who is not under the law of God, and the other, the son of

God who has the Spirit of God dwelling in him: "For the good that I would I do not: but the evil which I would not, that I do." There seem to be two of us, the one warring with the other—one who knows the right and the other who is struggling against it, one who wants to be the perfected man and the other who through limitation of one sort or another cannot achieve it.

When we come to the place of realizing that there is a son of God in us, but that the prodigal son of man is still struggling for survival, we begin to understand the warfare between the flesh and the Spirit. The prodigal, or Adamic man, out in the world using up his substance and finally sinking to the depths of degradation as symbolized by his eating with the swine, was none other than the son and heir who later wore the purple robe and jeweled ring. They were not two different men, but the selfsame man in two different states of consciousness.

As soon as we can begin to accept the principle that there is neither good nor evil in person, thing, or condition, that is, in any effect or appearance, in that moment the inner yielding begins which leads to the life by Grace, because we are now no longer in conflict with, or in opposition to, any person or thing. There is always the choice of accepting one way or the other, and the choice as to which way we accept is ours.

The goal of life now becomes the attainment of the conscious awareness of our true Self; or as it is stated in mystical literature that conscious union with God in which the little self disappears and the pure Self remains intact as our eternal and everlasting identity.

There is within every one of us the kingdom of God. There is within every one of us a capacity for living on earth without fighting, hating, or envying. But this we cannot do as human beings, and that is why we are told by our friends that this is a very impractical way of life—beautiful, of course, but very impractical.

The "I say unto you" of the Sermon on the Mount is possible only when people come to the realization that they are not living off one another or from one another or by human modes or means, but by "every word that proceedeth out of the mouth of God." The Sermon on the Mount is a way of life that is impossible for us as human beings to attain, unless we have contacted the divine faculties within us and are living through the Soul rather than through the body and mind. Then as we begin to accept the responsibility of loving our neighbor as ourselves and loving God supremely, acknowledging in true humility that of our own selves we can do nothing—that we cannot even be good because there is but one good, the Father, and nothing else is either good or evil—we are on the mystical path, the path of conscious communion with God.

In the Sermon on the Mount, which is the greatest message ever given to the world, two diametrically opposite ways of life are presented. Here is the *ye-have-heard-it-said-of-old* *way*, the way the world is *now* living, and here too is the *but-I-say-unto-you way*, the new dispensation of living by divine Grace.

"I say unto you" is a complete assurance that God is the creative, maintaining, and sustaining principle. It is the mystical way of life in which we are not the actor, the doer, or the be-er, but in which there is a transcendental Presence and Power which the Master called the Father within.

We live under the law and are in the ye-have-heard-it-said-of-old or the prodigal experience as long as we are in the mind-creation of the second chapter of Genesis. When we return to our original state of pure being, we no longer live under karmic law but under Grace—under the "I say unto you" of the Sermon on the Mount.

# CHAPTER XI

# I SAY UNTO YOU

For I say unto you, That except your righteousness shall exceed the righteousness of the scribes and Pharisees, ye shall in no case enter into the kingdom of heaven.

MATTHEW 5:20

In the Sermon on the Mount, the Master made a clear distinction between the Old Testament teaching, the ye-have-heard-it-said-of-old way, and the new teaching of *My kingdom* which is not of this world—something different from being merely a good person humanly, and living by the standard of two powers. Here was a complete departure from the old Hebraic teaching; here was a whole new standard which took no cognizance of either good or evil.

We can know how close we are to *My kingdom* by observing to what degree we still react to good and evil. How joyously do we react to the good and how much are we disturbed by the bad? In what measure are we becoming indifferent to either the human good or the human evil?

There is a spiritual kingdom, and dwelling in it would make us completely indifferent even to the good things of life. Only at the beginning of our journey on the spiritual path do we think that the ultimate goal is the improvement of our human experience, that doubling our income is a good demonstration or that having our heart, liver, or lungs function a little more normally—or even perfectly according to human standards—represents spiritual demonstration and is an indication of progress on the spiritual path.

The true demonstration that we should be seeking is not merely the increase of dollars or an improvement in health, as desirable as these are, but rather should it be a rebirth, an entrance into that state of consciousness which is the *My kingdom* not of this world.

If we want merely to be humanly happy, healthy, and wealthy, we should remain nominal Christians, because trying to follow the teaching of Christ Jesus demands a tremendous price, a strict and a disciplined way of life. True, there are inner joys untold and inner peace beyond the imagination, but for a long time there will be a Soul-stirring struggle with that little devil called *self*—a struggle with the personal sense of "I," "me," and "mine."

We are responsible to a large extent for our lives as we find them at this moment, not responsible in the sense that it is necessarily the mistakes that we have consciously or unconsciously made or our deliberate transgressions and offenses, as much as because of our ignorance of life and life's principles which has made us an easy prey to world beliefs. Had we been properly taught from infancy and had we possessed a knowledge of spiritual law, we would have learned how to avoid many of the discords in our experience. Certainly, the bulk of our trouble has been due to our ignorance of life, and even some of our good fortune may have come through what the world considers luck or fortuitous circumstances.

From our earliest years, the desirability of being a go-getter, having a strong personality, being dynamic, knowing what we want and going after it, and the importance of getting, achieving, and accomplishing have been impressed upon us, whereas those very qualities may be responsible for some of our problems because through these acquisitive traits of character we have undoubtedly violated spiritual law. Not only the bread that we have cast upon the waters has been gathered unto ourselves, but very often, depending upon the extent of our cleverness and oftentimes unscrupulousness, we have maneuvered so as to capture some that belongs to others, and in doing this, that violation of spiritual law was bound to react upon us. Similarly, whenever we have pushed or elbowed someone aside mentally or physically or reached out for that which is rightfully someone else's, in that degree have we also violated spiritual law.

Even that for which we have legally and legitimately struggled was sometimes the very thing that destroyed us because, inasmuch as we are infinite and, according to the teaching of the Master, have within us all that the Father has, any attempt to add to that infinity is in itself a violation of the law of God. To be spiritually attuned and live in accordance with the laws of God, we must begin with the realization that all that the Father has is embodied within us—the bread of life and the wine of inspiration—the whole kingdom of God is established within us. Then, instead of starting out in life with the idea of gaining, getting, or achieving, we would reverse that, and our attitude would be one of serving, giving, bestowing, sharing, and co-operating. We would be living out from our withinness in the confidence and assurance that our joy is in sharing and co-operating. In such a state of consciousness, our good on the human plane would be the reflex action of our giving and sharing.

Every time we believe that there is something or somebody to be gained or won—some name, some fame, some fortune—we are at that very moment in violation of the spiritual principle of life which is givingness. As the offspring of God, the Spirit of God made flesh, all that God is we are, and all that the Father has is ours. To believe otherwise would be to break that relationship of oneness in much the same way as the prodigal son did when, thinking and believing that what he had was his own even though given to him originally by his father, he lived his riotous life, spent and wasted his substance.

So it is with us, even if we begin by realizing that God is our wisdom, our supply, and God is our this, that, or the other thing, and then forget to continue acknowledging our Source and instead claim it and use it as if it were our own, often what we do is to deplete and exhaust that supply because in claiming anything as our own we thereby cut ourselves off from the Source, and such separation results in limitation.

In understanding God as the Source, there is nothing that we are spending—not strength, years, wisdom, substance, or life-force—because it was not ours to begin with. It is all pouring through us as we call upon it from an infinite Source. To believe in a limited supply is very much like gauging the water supply of a community by the amount of water in the pipes at any particular moment, forgetting that there is a reservoir close by and that that reservoir is constantly being replenished from the never-failing source of the rain and snow.

The conviction that it is our intelligence, our wisdom, our strength, our vitality, and our years that are being used stems from the ignorant belief that we of ourselves are something and that the length of our life can be determined by using that generally accepted threescore years and ten as a measure. Had we been taught from the beginning the lesson that the Master has so plainly given us of our true relationship to God—that it is not our life that is being lived but God's life; it is not our strength that is being used, but His strength; it is not our understanding or supply that is infinite but His; and that we are but the instruments through which God pours His life forth to glorify Himself—we would long ago have realized that it is our function to live, not as ailing, aging human beings, but as the image and likeness of God, drawing upon God for our daily wisdom, strength, and supply.

It will be no credit to you or to me if we live to be one hundred fifty, looking like fifty and in full possession of all our faculties, wits, intelligence, strength, and health. It will be God glorifying Himself by means of you and me, just as God glorifies Himself through the sun, the moon, and the stars. "The heavens declare the glory of God; and the firmament sheweth his handiwork." We do not praise and give credit to the stars for being beautiful or to the sun for being bright and warm, or to the moon for giving light. If we give glory to anything, we should give glory to God that He has expressed Himself in such a manner. So, whatever we show forth in the way of spiritual harmony, let us take no credit for it, but realize that through us God is showing forth His handiwork, God is glorifying Himself as our form, as our wisdom, and as our grace.

The Sermon on the Mount points up sharply these two ways of life: the ye-have-heard-it-said-by-them-from-old-time way—the getting, achieving, struggling for survival way—and the I-say-unto-you way—the letting, giving, and resting in My peace way.

Ye have heard that it was said by them of old time, Thou shalt not kill. . . .
But I say unto you, That whosoever is angry with his brother without a cause shall be in danger of the judgment.

MATTHEW 5:21, 22

To be obedient to the thou-shalt-not-kill edict is to possess the righteousness of the ye-have-heard-it-said-of-old way. Such was the righteousness of the scribes and Pharisees who were obedient to the law. Such is the righteousness of many of the "religious" people of today, for they also teach—every denomination teaches—"Thou shalt not kill." But the righteousness of those on the spiritual path has to be beyond that, it has to go beyond being angry with one's brother, beyond retaliation.

Ye have heard that it hath been said, An eye for an eye, and a tooth for a tooth. . . .

MATTHEW 5:38

If our sense of righteousness is of the brand that wants to be avenged for the wrongs that have been committed against us, again it can be likened to the righteousness of the scribes and Pharisees, that is, to some of the religionists of the world today. But listen to what "I say unto you"—I, the Christ:

Resist not evil. . . .
And if any man will sue thee at the law, and take away thy coat, let him have thy cloke also.

MATTHEW 5:39, 40

This is one of those sayings of the Master which the people of Jesus' day called "a hard saying," and one which today is considered *impractical*. If people are sued, they retaliate by a counter suit; if they are wronged, they go to great lengths—sometimes to any length—to establish their rights. Such is the righteousness of the scribes and Pharisees. But the Christ says unto us that we cannot resort to such means. If our property is taken away from us or if an attempt is made to take it away, we have to accept such loss with good grace; if we are harmed, we must seek no redress. It is a hard saying, but nevertheless the Christ says that we must stand still.

Ye have heard that it hath been said, Thou shalt love thy neighbour, and hate thine enemy.
But I say unto you, Love your enemies. . . .

MATTHEW 5:43, 44

This *I* within our own being—not a man two thousand years ago—this *I* says to us, "Love your enemies, bless them that curse you." If we are Christians in name alone, we may claim that we are living up to these "hard" sayings, but if we are practicing Christians, we cannot give only lip service to these teachings: We have to get up each day and *do* it.

And when thou prayest, thou shalt not be as the hypocrites are: for they love to pray standing in the synagogues and in the corners of the streets, that they may be seen of men.

MATTHEW 6:5

Jesus had a way of seeing through human nature, and in this statement he strips bare of pretense those people who gather in churches solely to be seen of men.

And he had a word also for the people who resort to and depend on affirmations:

But when ye pray, use not vain repetitions, as the heathen do: for they think that they shall be heard for their much speaking.

MATTHEW 6:7

The Master had an answer for everything. He knew that God is our Soul, closer than breathing and nearer than hands and feet; he knew that there is nothing going on within us that the Soul of us does not know. Therefore, while we may possibly hoodwink the man standing beside us, we certainly cannot fool the Man standing within us.

For if ye forgive men their trespasses, your heavenly Father will also forgive you:
But if ye forgive not men their trespasses, neither will your Father forgive your trespasses.

MATTHEW 6:14, 15

To live humanly is to forgive in one instance and withhold forgiveness in another; it is to judge, condemn, and criticize, to live the human way in which we might feel justified in retorting, "Well, look what he did—he deserved it." Jesus, however, brought to light a spiritual way of life which takes no cognizance of what anyone thinks, does, or is. He merely said, "Forgive."

Moreover when ye fast, be not, as the hypocrites, of a sad countenance: for they disfigure their faces, that they may appear unto men to fast.

MATTHEW 6:16

There again is the human desire not only to be good, but to want everybody to know about our goodness.

But thou, when thou fastest, anoint thine head, and wash thy face;
That thou appear not unto men to fast, but unto thy Father, which is in secret.

MATTHEW 6:17, 18

Here is Jesus' reversal of the whole human picture, and if we follow his teaching, we do not advertise our good, nor do we seek credit for it: We simply live up to our highest sense of right.

Lay not up for yourselves treasures upon earth, where moth and rust doth corrupt, and where thieves break through and steal:

But lay up for yourselves treasures in heaven, where neither moth nor rust doth corrupt, and where thieves do not break through nor steal:

For where your treasure is, there will your heart be also.

MATTHEW 6:19–21

The human way of life is to lay up treasures, and of course, the practical man reminds us of the importance of saving for the possibly dark days ahead, and there is no denying that if we have dissipated our assets or squandered our money, we may come upon the day when we wish we had been less prodigal. Our real treasure, however, is the spiritual wisdom we have garnered.

No man can serve two masters: for either he will hate the one, and love the other; or else he will hold to the one, and despise the other. Ye cannot serve God and mammon.

MATTHEW 6:24

We cannot live according to a human standard of life and at the same time reap the fruitage of the spiritual life: We cannot live according to an-eye-for-an-eye and a-tooth-for-a-tooth philosophy, nor depend upon treasures laid up where moth and rust corrupt; we cannot live according to the human code and at the same time pray to God for spiritual light, spiritual bread, spiritual wine, and spiritual water.

Take no thought for your life, what ye shall eat, or what ye shall drink; nor yet for your body, what ye shall put on. . . . (For after all these things do the Gentiles seek:). . . .

MATTHEW 6:25, 32

In the time of Jesus, the Gentiles were the pagans: They

were the ones who lived after the flesh; they were the ones who did as so many of us do today; they took thought—much thought—about what they were to eat, drink, and wear. But Jesus reminds us that the truly Christian life is a dependence upon the Infinite Invisible; it is a life lived with the understanding that the Soul within us is our bread, wine, and water, that that Soul is our intelligence, the strength of our body and that which renews the body, making it youthful and harmonious for the purpose of wholesome and fruitful living.

To live without taking thought is not sensible humanly, but as we find ourselves being fed from those inner waters of life eternal, our life is supported and maintained by the inner Soul-faculties. Living by the spiritual standard, we live what in Christian terminology is called the life by Grace. There is that within us which we call our Soul, the substance of our life, upon which we can draw as we would upon our checking account, but with this difference. With a checking account, we are limited to what we have deposited in the bank, but in the spiritual way of life we are limited only to what God has. We can draw upon our Soul for strength or wisdom, for skill in our profession or even in driving an automobile, in running a business or a household.

When the spiritual capacities have been developed, there is absolutely no limit to what can be accomplished because it is not we who accomplish it. God it is who does these things, God it is who goes out invisibly into this world and draws to us everything and everybody necessary for our experience, and we find ourselves drawn to the place where we should be at the right time, receiving that which we should have.

Paul called it living by the Christ, letting the Christ live our life, letting the Christ do all things—not through muscles, not through bank accounts, not by revenge, but through the Christ which strengthens us. To live by the Christ demands that we give up the personal sense of life with its reliance on physical force, human reasoning, and material resources.

In the Sermon on the Mount, are set forth two entirely different ways of life with no common meeting ground. The one is the ye-have-heard-it-said-of-old way exemplified by the righteousness of the scribes and Pharisees, which is the way of the great majority of human beings the world over. It is also the way of almost all religious teachings on earth today, except for those mystical teachings which rarely reach human consciousness because most people do not seek for a way of life which is such a radical departure from the conventional human mode of living; and therefore, except among those who follow the mystical path, little, or perhaps more correctly, nothing is known of the I-say-unto-you way of life.

The Master's great teaching in the Sermon on the Mount and in all the four Gospels is not one of weakness, expediency, or compromise; nor is it one of blindly and meekly letting the world do anything it wants to do to us and of our passively taking all the beating that it wants to give us. Rather is it one in which we resist not evil in the realization that the Father within is taking care of our interests.

To a person engrossed in materiality, enmeshed in and governed by that tyrannical master, the reasoning mind, this way of life would undoubtedly be quickly judged and condemned as totally and impossibly impractical. At first it does seem impractical, but let us stop for one moment and try to see why it is that we feel we must protect ourselves by battling and struggling mentally, physically, or prayerfully. Is not all this based on the erroneous premise that there are two powers in this world? If there were only one power, God, would there be anything to struggle against or to battle? It is true that if we judge according to what we see and hear, there are two powers. But upon what are we basing our judgment? Are we not judging solely by appearances? Are we not judging by the evidence before us? The Master warned us not to judge according to the appearance, but to judge righteous judgment. If we judge righteously, which means bearing witness not to what we see or hear but to what unfolds spiritually from within, we shall soon discover the miracle and the mystery of this teaching: There are not two powers—there is only one.

In the Sermon on the Mount, we are shown the human way of life as we have been living it, but we are also given a glimpse of the spiritual life which can be attained and which is the most practical way of life there is because it is a life lived by a spiritual principle, and that spiritual Principle is God—infinite, eternal, universal, omnipresent, omnipotent, and omniscient.

At some period in our lives, we must all come to an actual demonstrable experience of that Presence which Jesus called the Father within. Not only must we individually experience this Presence, but we must contribute in every way possible to making it a part of world experience.

There are faint rumblings of a new understanding among nations. Not too many years ago the only way of settling international disputes was by war. The conference table was tried by a few, but usually failed because lurking in men's minds was the thought that if talk proved ineffectual, there was always the possibility of calling out the army and navy, but to what can nations resort in this day of nuclear fission? Since everybody realizes that civilization could never survive an atomic war, those in responsible positions are now seeking for some other solution to world tensions. Some of them have even come to the place where they are wont to censure their allies if they resort to violence and forgo the conference table. Regardless of how much right seems to be on any nation's side, the world is slowly ceasing to tolerate the use of force, even if temporarily a nation loses by virtue of failing to use physical might. That is the first toddling step toward the mode of life advocated in the Sermon on the Mount.

Years and years and years ago, before ever The Infinite Way was dreamed of, I saw that the solution to all human problems rested in the ability not to fight back, not to fight error, but on the ability to rest in the one Power. Once we are able to do that, we are practicing the Sermon on the Mount and living the spiritual life, because then there is no more need to seek good health than to get rid of bad health; there is no more need to seek supply than to run away from lack: We stand still in divine Being, not in human being.

A human being needs many things: He must be healed, he must be supplied; he must have his lot improved. Not so the child of God. The child of God is sustained by the Father within. When we have risen above hate and love to the point where we pray equally and sincerely for the unjust as well as the just, then we have risen above the pairs of opposites. Then we are approaching the I-say-unto-you consciousness of the Sermon on the Mount.

That is the secret of the Sermon on the Mount. It takes us away from both health and no-health, supply and no-supply into that world of the first chapter of Genesis where we judge not at all whether it is health or not health, supply or not supply, but whether we stand in that Spirit. In other words, we return to the first chapter of Genesis.

# CHAPTER XII

# RESIST NOT

To live the spiritual life means to live above the human sense of life, to live without recourse to human modes and means, that is, to live by the Christ. It means never to return evil for evil, never to pray or hope or wish or desire that another suffer for his offense—even his offense to us—never to desire to recoup our losses, which is the human way of life and, under our laws, legal. But legal or not, this is not the way of the Christ. True, if someone defrauds us, it is considered legitimate, proper, and right to sue him, but such procedure is not spiritual.

And if any man will sue thee at the law, and take away thy coat, let him have thy cloke also.

MATTHEW 5:40

If someone were to counsel us, "I say to you, you must stop your lawsuits. If anybody wants to take your property, let him have it; if he wants your home, let him take it; if he takes your automobile, let him have it; and if he decides to come in and get your jewelry, let him have that too, and then look around and see if you cannot give him a few extra things

131

in addition to what he already has taken," such advice would seem contrary to all reason.

But that is what Jesus tells us to do in the fifth chapter of the Gospel of Matthew, and at this moment we have no way of knowing whether he was right or wrong. We have no way of knowing whether we might not benefit twice over by obeying that very command because most of us have not tried the resist-not-evil way of life; and moreover, until we have reached that state of consciousness, it would probably be very unwise for us to try it.

At first thought, such a teaching might seem to mean that we are to let anybody and everybody walk all over us, defraud and take from us all that we have while we are just the sweet gentle things that permit ourselves to be walked on. But Jesus the Christ never meant that. What he meant was that we should not retaliate humanly, but he did not say what would happen spiritually if his advice were followed. He does not say a single word about what God will do for us when we stop doing for ourselves. He does not explain how the problem will be worked out without invoking the law of "an eye for an eye and a tooth for a tooth." The implication, however, is that a spiritual Presence comes to our rescue to lift us up above injustice and dishonesty. Is it really possible for anyone to defraud us if we stand on our spiritual identity as the child of God?

When the soldiers came to seize the Master in the Garden and the sword was drawn in his defense, Jesus refused to permit his disciples to defend him, saying, "Put up again thy sword into his place: for all they that take the sword shall perish with the sword." To material sense, that would seem as if he were giving them *carte blanche* to drag him away and do whatever they wanted to do with him. But he was not doing that at all. Instead, he was realizing, "I have an Infinite Invisible upon which I rely. I have a divine Something that knoweth my need before I do, and it is Its good pleasure to give me the kingdom." In that complete reliance he rested.

"Resist not evil" sounds like the most foolish and impractical of human teachings, yet it is the wisest and most practical of spiritual principles. Those who attain a state of consciousness in which they can let the enemy come at them with the armor of the world—with spears, knives, guns, or lawsuits—and can stand in complete confidence with no resistance, can never lose, any more than could David lose his skirmish with Goliath, or than could the Hebrews, who were so greatly outnumbered by the enemy, lose their battle.

As long as we resist evil, we are not living under Grace but under the law; and the very knife that we throw at another will boomerang to pierce us in the chest, all in a blinding flash and out of nowhere. There is no way for Grace to descend upon us if we are indulging the human way of life. We can pray for Grace for a million years, but it will not come to us until we give up using the weapons of the world and arrive at Job's understanding that He "hangeth the earth upon nothing." Then if we are willing to lean back on that nothingness, the Spirit rushes in to pick us up and carry us forward, appearing in and as whatever form may be necessary.

The Master reveals the basic karmic law of *as ye sow, so shall ye reap*, but he also makes plain the one sure and certain way to rise above the law of cause and effect, and that is not to set in motion a cause—to do nothing, think nothing, and be nothing *of ourselves*. For example, if we pray with some object or purpose in mind, we are likely to produce an effect in accordance with the cause which we set up. But if we were to pray without an object, solely for the realization of God, then we would not have set up a cause, and there could be no effect. There would only be God Itself appearing as the harmony of our existence.

So it is that if we do not take up the weapons of defense in our behalf, we cannot be injured by those weapons. If we do not mete out justice according to human standards, then human justice cannot come back at us. Whatever it is that we bind, that is what is bound to us; whatever we loose, that is what is loosed. We are the ones who determine that, and when we relinquish the thoughts and things of this world and live in a continuous desire to know God aright, leaving all other considerations aside, then when God is realized, God appears in our experience as a perfected life.

Everything that we see, hear, taste, touch, or smell exists as an effect, but the moment that we perceive that there is neither good nor evil in effect, we lose our fear of any and every effect. We cannot fear something that has no more power for good or for evil than has a glass of pure water. We not only cannot fear a glass of pure water—we cannot even love it. We can enjoy and benefit by it, but there is nobody yet who has ever fallen in love with a glass of water or hated it or feared it. We just take it as it is, for what it is—a glass of water.

The Master had that same attitude toward leprosy: He did not hate it and he did not fear it, and he certainly did not love it. He went up and touched it, showing by that action that he had risen above the belief of good and evil. For him, it had no power.

It is possible for us to rise above the law of cause and effect —but only when the world's weapons have been given up, only when our life is lived not by bread alone but by every word that proceeds out of the mouth of God. When we are not thinking of food or money or climate or any effect as constituting our security and when we realize that our real life is sustained by the word of God, we are living the spiritual life with no dependence on human beings, on human investments, or human positions—not throwing them away or casting them out of our life, but realizing that they are the added things in life, part of God's grace made manifest, and therefore there is no thought whatsoever of fear should they be taken from us.

If our dependence is on the material way of life, then when those reliances are swept away, we are indeed lost. No one is ever lost, however, who practices the spiritual way of life. who no longer takes up the sword in his own defense, whether it be the sword of a lawsuit or a bombproof shelter, who no longer relies on force—not even on forceful arguments—but rather rests quietly at the center of his being and lets the Infinite Invisible be his defense and his offense if necessary. This Infinite Invisible will never destroy any person, but It will destroy evil influences or thoughts, beliefs or acts that may try to manifest through the person.

Individually, we develop the state of consciousness that lives without using power and which finally brings our particular world into the orbit of no-power by understanding that nothing that exists as person, place, thing, circumstance, or condition is imbued with the power for good or for evil. There is no power for good or for evil, because *there is no power*. Nothing is power, and nobody is power: God alone is a creative, maintaining, and sustaining power which operates without any help from us. *God alone is power, and we are the instruments through which, and as which, It flows, but God alone is, and always remains, the only power.*

The Master understood this clearly when he said, "Why callest thou me good? . . . I can of mine own self do nothing. . . . the Father that dwelleth in me, he doeth the works." So it is with us. Power is not really given to us, but if we come to a state of mind in which we are so cradled in the Spirit that we do not resist the seeming error by denying, fighting, or trying to destroy it, we too shall witness the wondrous things which the Father within performs.

A consciousness must be built in which the response to any problem that is presented to us is, "Look, here it is in my mind. I'm looking at it. It isn't benefiting me; it isn't hurting me. It is a shadow. I know the world has said that this thing is a power, that it can kill, destroy, or weaken, but I say it is a shadow because in a God-created world, it cannot be a power, and I do not need any power—I do not even need a power to destroy it or overcome it or remove it."

Human existence is based on a belief or trust in two powers, and even religion is based on the power of God over evil; but in heaven there are no powers of good or of evil: There is only God Itself, living Its own life as you and as me, and as a heavenly universe. The very moment we can demonstrate the Master's teaching of *resist not evil*, we shall no longer spend our days as most of the world is doing, chasing, searching, and begging for a power to do something, and competing with everybody else in the world. When we realize this new principle—not a new power but a new principle, a new dimension of life—we live in a world where there is no competition and in a universe where men do not fight one another.

Watch the transformation of your own world as you bring yourself inwardly to the feeling that you do not want to oppose or use a power against anybody or anything.

"Resist not evil." At first it may be that somebody will want to take every last dollar you have in the world, but he cannot permanently deprive you of one dime because faster than he can deprive you of it, it will be returned to you in some way, so that it will not be long before you will have as much as you had before and probably twelve baskets full left over; whereas if you struggle to hold on to it, you may find yourself with less.

Wars and lawsuits result from the conviction that possessions—whether of land, money, or persons—must be held tightly within the owner's grasp at whatever price, even if it arouses envy, jealousy, and hatred. When any form of evil or danger threatens, immediately the law of self-preservation goes to work, which instinctively causes us to raise our hands or make a fist; and if we are students of metaphysics, we quickly set up a mental wall of defense resorting to affirmations and denials such as, "It isn't true. It isn't so. There is no life in matter. God is all." There is a resistance to the error as if it were a power, whereas the truth is, it is only "an arm of flesh." Such an attitude leaves us without any feeling of needing to overcome, rise above, or destroy anything.

The physical resistance of fist or sword and the mental resistance of affirmations and denials are practically the same thing, but rising above the physical and the mental into the spiritual realm brings us to that new dimension where there is no power, where there is no good over evil, where every situation is met by resting in the Spirit.

It is only the Spirit of God in us that enables us to rise above seeking revenge, or wanting to defend ourselves from slander, scandal, or rumors. When we can refuse to yield to the temptation to justify or defend ourselves, when we can smile and say, "If you believe it, I am sorry for you," and let it go at that, then we are trusting the Christ to make the necessary adjustments and bring to us the defense which the Master promised: "Settle it therefore in your hearts, not to meditate before what ye shall answer: For I will give you a mouth and wisdom, which all your adversaries shall not be able to gainsay nor resist." We do not have to plan in advance what we are going to say; we do not have to be a clever attorney for ourselves, but only wait until we are before the judge, open our mouth, and hear the Spirit speak through us.

Let us learn to sit quietly, resting in the realization that underneath are "the everlasting arms," and that no amount of praying will put those everlasting arms there: They are already underneath us. If it is necessary as a reminder, whenever problems are brought to our attention for solution, we should close our eyes and remember what Jesus said to Peter, "Put up again thy sword into his place."

All these discordant pictures that we see round about us are just mental images in thought, shadows on a screen. We must learn not to be afraid to look at them and understand that they have no more substance than the men and women on a moving picture screen and no more power than the bullets that are fired into, and through, our television sets, but which never crack the set open. They make a great deal of noise, but they are nothing but shadows; and one day, as we look into our mind, we shall see and understand that there are these mental images or pictures of what is called life and that they are all taking place inside, not outside, our mind. What we see is not the event itself, nor the person involved: It is a mental concept which we have drawn and are entertaining of the event or person.

When we realize that the problem presenting itself to us is not a God-created spiritual entity, but a mental concept without cause or reality—without presence, power, or substance—then in the realization of God as the creative, maintaining, and sustaining Principle of all that truly is, we already have all the God-power needed, without turning to God to do anything about it.

It is not necessary to overcome hate, fear, jealousy, or resentment, but it *is* necessary to sit down, close the eyes, and realize, "These are mental images in thought. These are projected states of thought out of the vast mental illusion." Then by abiding in an inner peace, they are dissolved. They are not destroyed because there is nothing to be destroyed; there is no substance to them and they have no more reality than the pictures on our television screen. True, back of the moving picture there is a real picture with substance, just as behind every belief, theory, or false picture that is presented to us, there is a reality; but the reality is distorted in the picture, and it is that distortion that is dissolved as the reality appears.

The conditioned mind forms our problems, and there are times when that mind might form an answer to the problem, but that is not what we are seeking. What we want is a higher capacity than the human mind, and so now, without calling upon the thinking process, we let our mind be an instrument through which the Soul can reveal Itself.

A problem can exist only in the mind. But if we make of our mind a vacuum, if there are no thoughts in it, where would our problem be? There is then no problem, and in place of the problem the truth or reality rushes in.

If, instead of fighting a problem, we are willing to admit that to all appearances this problem seems to be overwhelming and turn within asking to have the reality revealed, then we are not trying to rise above or destroy the problem. We are merely trying to understand—not understand the problem, but understand the reality behind the problem. If we can be perfectly quiet and perfectly still with no attempt to overcome, destroy, remove, or escape from any situation or condition, the flow of the Spirit will rush in and there will be freedom.

When error is presented in any form, there is a tendency to set up a wall against it, and in doing that, the opportunity to make the demonstration is lost because no wall is needed. Do not put up a wall against evil; do not put up a defense: Understand that no external thing has power, not even the good things. All good is in Spirit, or Consciousness, not in the things that Consciousness produces.

Come with me now into an inner stillness in which we do not resort to any power to do anything. We resist not evil and let evil do anything it wants to do, while we neither deny nor affirm. We will not seek God and we will not fear a devil, but sit at peace, with no struggle, no strife, no battle:

"The Lord is my shepherd. . . . He maketh me to lie down in green pastures: he leadeth me beside the still waters: He prepareth a table before me in the presence of mine enemies." He performeth that which is given me to do; He performeth that which concerneth me.

I live and move and have my being in God; therefore, I need not fear; I need not fight because the battle is not mine.

"Where the Spirit of the Lord is, there is liberty"—no struggle, only peace. "Peace . . . my peace I give unto you: not as the world giveth," not a peace that comes from destroying the neighboring country or people, not a peace that comes from having a stockpile of atomic bombs, but My peace. Nothing can destroy me, nothing can harm me, for there is nothing but My peace.

Those who live by the sword, even a mental sword, shall die by the sword. So put it up. Stop defending yourself. In every prayer and in every meditation—in every treatment—

remind yourself to put up your sword. When we no longer use human weapons, physical or mental, we relax, not into letting the world do what it wants with us, but into that Spirit which is within us in order to let It take over and govern our experience.

The Sermon on the Mount gives us a choice between two ways of life—the law or Grace. If we choose the law, we will probably have a little easier time of it because we shall be conforming to common practice, going along with the crowd, and in some measure we may for a time benefit, until the day of retribution comes. On the other hand, if we attempt to live by Grace, we shall find ourselves out of step with this world, and we may temporarily suffer injustices that we do not deserve. In the final analysis, however, we find that we have come under God's grace, God's government, and God's protection. God's will and not the will of man is being done in us. And that is an entirely different life.

# CHAPTER XIII

# THE FATHER WHICH SEETH IN SECRET

And when thou prayest, thou shalt not be as the hypocrites are: for they love to pray standing in the synagogues and in the corners of the streets, that they may be seen of men. Verily I say unto you, They have their reward.

But thou, when thou prayest, enter into thy closet, and when thou hast shut thy door, pray to thy Father which is in secret; and thy Father which seeth in secret shall reward thee openly.

MATTHEW 6:5, 6

These words of the Master must come as a shock to us when we realize how many people believe that their most effective prayers are those said in church. How many times have we, ourselves, prayed in public, forgetting that, according to Jesus, prayer must be practiced in secret. Of old, the Pharisees and the scribes prayed in public in much the same manner as do most of the people of our world today, and for their much praying, they received the praise of their neighbors: There is only one thing they lost—God's grace.

When our prayers become a matter of public utterance, we are inflating our ego, trying to make something of ourselves, setting out to glorify ourselves, not realizing that thereby we sacrifice the reward of the Father and separate ourselves from the very blessings we are seeking. Anything

141

that glorifies ourselves or attempts to make the world believe that we are something of ourselves tends to separate us from the love of God. The whole teaching of the Master is, "I can of mine self do nothing . . . the Father that dwelleth in me, he doeth the works. . . . My doctrine is not mine, but his that sent me."

This injunction to pray in secret does not mean that we cannot unite with others in prayer or meet in church or temple for the purpose of prayer because Jesus also taught that "where two or three are gathered together in my name, there am I in the midst of them." His intent was that we should not attend church because it is the accepted thing to do—fashionable or politic—or because our neighbors would gossip about us if we were not there. Our reason for going to church should be because of a desire to unite in a holy atmosphere in silent and secret prayer with other devoted followers of the spiritual way of life for the purpose of being in communion with God, in order that we may receive the baptism of the Holy Ghost.

Jesus also reminds us not to pray in holy mountains, nor yet in that Temple in Jerusalem, again meaning that we are not to expect any greater realization of the Presence in holy mountains or in temples than we would find if we were praying in our garden or at home or in our living room, because "the kingdom of God cometh not with observation: Neither shall they say, Lo here! or, Lo there! for, behold, the kingdom of God is within" us. The only way we can pray without ceasing is to pray wherever we are—in the home, on the street, in the air, under the water, in church or out.

Prayer itself should never be a public display, nor for the purpose of being heard or seen of men. Prayer is a secret and a sacred experience, and, therefore, it must take place within the realm of our own consciousness, and then "the Father that seeth in secret" will reward us openly.

It is only after we begin the practice of secret prayer that we learn the efficacy of true prayer and begin to observe the changes that take place in our lives when we have periods every day for retiring to some quiet place where we can enter into a peaceful Silence, and there in secrecy commune with God. The Master taught that our prayers must be addressed to the Father that is within us, and there is no way to reach that center where God is except when we are quiet, peaceful, and serene within. So it becomes necessary to go into the closet, close the door of the sanctuary, and shut out the sounds and sights of the senses that we may touch that Center. Every thought that takes place within our consciousness reaches the throne of God and returns to us. It does not have to be seen or heard. There is only one way in which it can be measured—it must be sacred and unselfish:

*Right here within my own being is the Father, and this Father knows what thoughts I have; this Father knows the meditations of my heart; this Father knows whether I act from a standpoint of purity or from self-interest and hypocrisy.*

Within us are the issues of life, and they are decided there. Within us is the entire kingdom of God. That means that within us is the entire kingdom of immortality, eternality, virtue, prosperity, harmony, health, wholeness, completeness, and fulfillment. In our human selfhood, we can never bring that forth because as a human being we are living in terms of effect and not cause, but when a human being learns to make contact with his Source, he is then drawing on the Invisible and is back in Eden.

Only by abiding in the inner sanctuary can the return to the Father's house be accomplished, because in meditation the ego or personal sense of "I"—that Adam who lives by the sweat of his brow—is still. It is not claiming power, understanding, or wisdom. On the contrary, it is taking an attitude of humility, as if to say, "I am insufficient, incomplete, inharmonious; and so now I turn to the Source of my being, to That which is greater than I." By our stillness, we indicate our humility.

Customary prayer makes one superior to God because it tells God what it wants and usually when it wants it. It sets up the ego because it dares to try to influence God in one's behalf or in behalf of another. But in the silence of meditation, the prayer is:

*I do not ask You to serve my purpose, to do my will or my wish or my bidding. I am Your servant—do what You will with me. Teach me, feed me, direct me. You are closer to me than breathing. You know my needs, and it is Your good pleasure to give me the kingdom. Therefore I wait upon You.*

In this waiting, a vacuum is created, and the ego is in abeyance. The personal sense of self with its desires, wishes, hopes, and ambitions fades away, and then there is room for that transcendental spark to be kindled. There must be humility, before the Spirit of the Lord can be upon us. So it is that when we pray in secret, realizing our oneness with the Father and that, because of that oneness, all that the Father has is ours by divine inheritance and, therefore, it is our Father's good pleasure to give us the kingdom, we then need no longer look to any man for reward, compensation, gratitude, co-operation, or affection. When we understand our relationship with the Father, we learn to mold every thought and deed in accordance with His will.

The nature and purpose of secret prayer is little understood in the religious life of men and women today. Secrecy, however, is as potent as silence. Actually, it is the key to spiritual success, and without secrecy, spiritual demonstration is impossible.

Take heed that ye do not your alms before men, to be seen of them: otherwise ye have no reward of your Father which is in heaven.

Therefore when thou doest thine alms, do not sound a trumpet before thee, as the hypocrites do in the synagogues and in the streets, that they may have glory of men. Verily I say unto you, They have their reward.

MATTHEW 6:1, 2

Is not that a plain enough statement? And yet how many people in the world do their charity before men, have their generosity published in the newspapers, on the church bulletin board, or somewhere else where some neighbor, fellow citizen, or business associate needing to be impressed can see and tell them and others of their nobility and great contribution to the community, and possibly add what good Christians they are. But Jesus said of this practice, "Ye have no reward of your Father which is in heaven."

But when thou doest alms, let not thy left hand know what thy right hand doeth:
That thine alms may be in secret: and thy Father which seeth in secret himself shall reward thee openly.

MATTHEW 6:3, 4

The Father within us is our very own Soul, and anything that we do, our Soul knows; and if we do it in silence and in secrecy, He knows how to reward us openly. But when we do anything of a good nature and do it openly, there is first of all the implication that we are doing it, which is not true since God is the author of all good works and we are at best instruments or transparencies through which God's grace is appearing. Moreover, subconsciously we want others to be aware of our good works and to praise, admire, or thank us for our generosity and philanthropy as if we of ourselves were good.

When, however, we do our alms secretly, the personal sense of self is entirely absent, and God alone witnesses our good works. Any act of good performed secretly and sacredly attests to the absence of personal sense and the presence of God.

Moreover when ye fast, be not, as the hypocrites, of a sad countenance: for they disfigure their faces, that they may appear unto men to fast. Verily I say unto you, They have their reward.

But thou, when thou fastest, anoint thine head, and wash thy face;

That thou appear not unto men to fast, but unto thy Father which is in secret: and thy Father, which seeth in secret, shall reward thee openly.

MATTHEW 6:16–18

Let us not wear our spiritual heart on our sleeve: Let us not boast to men that we have found the secret of communion with the Source of life. Let us not expose our spiritual pearls to those unprepared to receive them, for in so doing they may be lost or trampled upon. Let our light shine by its fruitage rather than be flaunted before men and obscured by a veil of words.

It is not selfish to keep our relationship with God secret, because our light will shine to those prepared to see light, our wisdom will be heard by those who have ears to hear—even that which is imparted without words or thoughts.

The spiritual fast is an inward communing with God while abstaining from words or thoughts. It is an abiding in God unobserved by those around us. It is prayer in its highest sense in that it is a refraining from seeking anything of God, yet it is an awareness of God's grace freely flowing.

A teaching on such a high level of consciousness can never be understood by the human reasoning mind and, therefore, can be obeyed only by those whose goal is spiritual realization. How seldom are these esoteric teachings of Jesus on secrecy openly taught! How seldom is it recognized that there is a spiritual center in every person which is referred to in such revelations as, "Son, thou art ever with me, and all that I have is thine," or "I will never leave thee, nor forsake thee," or "I am with you alway, even unto the end of the world."

How many of us understand the mystery of these teachings? How many of us know that the *I* is literally in the midst of us and that that *I* that seeth in secret rewardeth us openly? By contemplation and meditation, we must solve the mystery of the spiritual life, and this we can do only when secretly and sacredly contemplating the nature of the Infinite Invisible which is closer to us than breathing. We must never believe that the mysteries of God will be revealed to us in the midst of the noise and clamor of discussion, argument, or theorizing. The hidden mysteries are not hidden from those who understand and obey the teaching of the Sermon on the Mount.

# CHAPTER XIV

# WHEN YE PRAY

For centuries the world has believed that merely voicing words in an attempt to reach God was sufficient to bring the power and the presence of God into daily experience. For hundreds of years, millions, even billions, of people all over the world have prayed for wars to cease, famine to be wiped off the earth, and disease to be healed—but all these have continued unabated.

No one experiences answered prayer when he prays merely with his mind, relying wholly on words and thoughts, because there is then no opportunity for the Spirit to break through into expression. Regardless of what form prayer may take, there is no connecting link with God until there is a conscious awareness of His presence.

But when ye pray, use not vain repetitions, as the heathen do: for they think that they shall be heard for their much speaking.

MATTHEW 6:7

Many of us have been guilty of using vain repetitions,

thinking that we are praying when in reality all we have been doing is repeating over and over again somebody else's man-made prayer. Even the repetition of as great a prayer as the Lord's Prayer, if recited with the idea that the mere rehearsal of its words has power, is not effective prayer because anything that is thought, spoken, or written is but an effect—and how can the power of God be in an effect? Does not all Scripture state that there is no power but the One, there is no God but one?

Prayer that is made up of words and thoughts cannot and does not reach God, and therefore remains unanswered. The prayers that are answered are those deep within a person when no words and no thoughts are present, but when there is a hunger, a desire, or a need that is beyond words. In that intense longing, God is reached.

The absence of fruitage in prayer merely bears witness to our failure to go deep enough into our consciousness to make contact with the Presence which is always there and which is ever available. God is not to be found on the surface of men's minds; God is not to be found through the intellect; God is not to be found except through deep prayer, a heart-hunger for God, a deep desire to know Him aright.

Prayer must be a desire for *spiritual* fulfillment. Through seeking first the kingdom of God, giving up hope of gaining any thing, and being satisfied to let the things be added unto us, we open ourselves to fulfillment. Who of us can know where spiritual fulfillment will lead or leave us? It may leave us in our present work or present mode of living, or it may lead us into new activities and an entirely new life.

In praying, however, it is important that we leave behind all our preconceived notions or ideas of what we want—our hopes, aims, ambitions, and desires—because there is no assurance that God will fulfill them on our terms. If we hope to see the fruitage of answered prayer, we must remember not to pray for anything at all that we think we need or that the world needs, but let our prayer be an inner stillness in which God's word flows into us reminding us, "Son . . . all that I have is thine." When God speaks His word, there will be no doubt of Its truth, and there will be no interval of barrenness between God's word and Its fulfillment.

As "joint-heirs with Christ," untold riches of the Spirit will be poured upon us in abundance, but no man knows what things God has stored up for those who love God's will and God's way.

> Eye hath not seen, nor ear heard, neither have entered into the heart of man, the things which God hath prepared for them that love him.
>
> I CORINTHIANS 2:9

Man cannot know what the divine plan holds for him because man can only measure good by an increase of what he already possesses. Whether it is dollars or horses he has, accumulating more of what to him represents good is his only way of evaluating good. These things, however, bear no relationship at all to real good, because no man can define what good actually is. No one can know the treasures that are stored up within himself until he turns to God in the realization that, whatever form it may take, God's grace is his sufficiency in all things, and until he is willing to follow in whatever way his good is unfolded and revealed even though that way may temporarily be a complete reversal or turning upside down of his human life, his hopes and activities.

Probably there is no one reading this book who has not already found that he is glad he did not receive many of the things for which he prayed so insistently. Therefore, it should not be too difficult to pray, "Not my will but Thine be done in me. Thou art the all-knowing, infinite wisdom and intelligence of the universe, and I surrender myself—I surrender my hopes and desires, my fears, my aims and ambitions—into Thy hand." Thus we make of our prayer an emptiness of self.

To bring ourselves as an empty vessel to God and let God fill that vessel is the highest form of prayer. Let us not take our finite views of what is good and what is bad to God, nor take our human hopes and ambitions to Him, but let us go to God as if we really trusted Him more than we would trust our own mother, trusted Him as the divine Love and the divine Wisdom of this world, which in truth He is.

When we do that, we are children of God, but as long as we are doing all the talking—telling, asking, pleading, beseeching, advising God—we are mortals, and our prayer does not reach God. Our prayers reach God only when we permit ourselves to be empty vessels, when our full faith and trust is "Thy will be done in me, Thy grace, Thy peace," and then wait in Silence, completely empty as the word of God comes to us and fills us, fulfills Itself and Its plan in us.

The reason for so much unhappiness is that many people are not fulfilling their own idea of themselves, much less God's idea. As human beings, a great many people are misfits. Scarcely a person on earth, regardless of how exalted his position, is fulfilling his true destiny on earth. Usually, he is either fulfilling a destiny that he has chosen for himself or one that circumstances have thrust upon him.

And so it is that if we are among those who are fulfilling some niche in life into which we have been thrown through circumstances beyond our control or in which we have placed ourselves through ignorance, certainly we need the prayer of fulfillment which is the prayer of emptiness. We need to learn how to release the whole situation into God, willingly admitting, "Look, I certainly have messed up this life of mine so far. Let me give up and You take over." Then we may be amazed at how the miracle begins to work in us and how quickly what we had thought of as our destiny changes.

There is no other way to pray. When we pray in that way, we are praying to the infinite Wisdom of the universe, trusting divine Love to fulfill Itself in us. As long as we are advising, suggesting, or outlining to God, or even hoping that God will act according to our personal wishes, we are not praying or going to God, but to our own mind. That is no way to pray. Rather should we surrender ourselves to God so that God's will for us may fulfill Itself, that whatever it was for which we were born—and we were all born for a purpose or we would not be here—may be fulfilled.

Regardless of how painful or difficult it may be at first to go to God without a word or a thought, a direction, a hope, a fear, or an ambition, this emptiness of self is worth achieving even if it takes time. When we reach that point, we shall find what a glorious thing it is not to have to plan our day or our next year, and yet at the same time be assured that every day of the year will be a day of fulfillment because it is God's day, and we have nothing to do with it except to be beholders of God at work. That which divinely decreed us to do it will fulfill it. He fulfills the days and He fulfills the nights as long as we are empty enough of words and are not injecting some human thought conceived in our mind.

When we begin to meditate, it is natural to think some thoughts, but let us be certain in our minds that we are not asking God for anything:

*I come here for prayer and meditation in the full knowledge that I am not going to a person, although the relationship between God and me is as personal as that between father and son or mother and son, but I am turning to the Spirit of wisdom and love whose will it is that I bear fruit richly.*

*I am not entering the presence of God in order to enlighten God. I am not going to God to present my views to Him, hoping to tell Him more than He already knows or to tell Him what is good for me to have. I do not expect through this period of prayer and communion to influence God in my behalf.*

*I turn to God that He may fill me full of Himself, fill me full of His wisdom, His peace and glory, and make me a fitting instrument on earth for His love.*

In this way we empty ourselves—we empty the old bottles of the old wine—making of ourselves a nothingness, without desire, hope, ambition, or fear; and in such a state of receptivity, we open the way for the Spirit of God to work in and through us in accordance with His plan and design.

God is hidden under hundreds of generations of mortality. God is hidden under hundreds of generations of people steeped in spiritual ignorance. God is hidden under all the layers of humanness, self-righteousness, self-protection, under all the *selfs* that we have built around and within ourselves making it almost impossible for us to reach Him. How then are we going to reach God? How, but in quietness and in confidence, in the stillness and the Silence? How, but by learning to abide in a quietness within, by being still? Then we shall contact the divine Selfhood which is within our own being, and when we establish contact with It, we will be in communion with the Father within just as the Master was.

How much praying has been done to a God somewhere other than within us! Yet the Master set the example by praying only to the Father within, crediting everything to the Father and turning in every situation to that withinness— whether it was the feeding of the multitudes or their healing.

Sooner or later we must all make contact with that Father, the Christ of our own being, with the Son of God within us. The Son of God constitutes our real being; the Son of God is the very life, mind, and Soul of us. The son of man has to learn to commune with the Son of God within, until the two become one, and then the son of man realizes, "I am never alone. I am never alone. Where I am, God is; where God is, I am."

The word of God received in our consciousness is the healing agency—quick and sharp and powerful. But the word of God must be *received*; it must not be a mere repetition of words because it is not our rehearsal of these truths that reveals God's presence and power, even though these truths do form the foundation on which we rest until the word of God bursts into our consciousness with some message such as, "Thou art free," or "Son . . . all that I have is thine," or "Thou art my beloved." Sometimes It says nothing at all, but we feel the inflow of peace and warmth throughout our whole system, or a smile coming to our face as much as to say, "How could I ever have believed that there is reality to this trouble?" When that inflow comes, which is really an inflow coming to our outer senses from the Father within, harmony is established, and healing takes place, whether for ourselves or for others.

To attain this, however, it is necessary first of all to stop turning to God as if there were a God somewhere waiting for our picayune little troubles to be brought to His throne to be taken care of. We must stop believing that God is withholding some good from us and that by some form of treatment, prayer, sacrifice, or coercion, we are going to get God to do what God is not already doing. All that nonsense must be given up, and we must turn to God in the sense of *Is*:

*God is, and I am not turning to God to do anything that God is not doing. I am standing on the Is-ness of God and realizing that where I am, God's grace is my sufficiency in all things.*

"Where the Spirit of the Lord is, there is liberty." And where is that Spirit? Wherever we acknowledge Him in all our ways; wherever we acquaint now ourselves with Him and are at peace; wherever we learn to sit in quietness and stillness—that is where the Spirit of the Lord is; and where that Spirit is, there is liberty and freedom from all forms of bondage—physical, moral, and financial.

As we learn to listen and develop a state of receptivity, eventually we arrive at that place where the flow begins to come from within. Neither written nor spoken truth can bring God into our lives. The written or the spoken word gives us a foundation upon which to rest while we are awaiting the realization of God's grace, but only when the Spirit moves upon us do the mighty works take place.

The words we speak are not power, nor are the thoughts we think, but if we sit in a complete quiet in the thundering Silence, and keep our "mind stayed on Thee," eventually we arrive at a place where thoughts do not come any more and, in a few moments, we begin to feel this inner peace that is known as realization.

Prayer is our contact with God. It is the means through which God's grace performs Its miracles in our experience. But prayer must be a listening attitude. It must be a willingness that the Spirit of God fill us and perform Its functions in us and through us.

# CHAPTER XV

# AS WE FORGIVE

F or nearly two thousand years the world has prayed, "Forgive us our debts, as we forgive our debtors," unaware perhaps that this teaching represents the very core, the very heart and soul, of the good life. Over and over again Jesus extols the virtues of forgiveness.

Therefore if thou bring thy gift to the altar, and there rememberest that thy brother hath ought against thee;
Leave there thy gift before the altar, and go thy way; first be reconciled to thy brother, and then come and offer thy gift. . . .
But if ye forgive not men their trespasses, neither will your Father forgive your trespasses.

MATTHEW 5:23, 24; 6:15

Does this not plainly state that as long as any malice, envy, jealousy, revenge, or hatred is entertained in consciousness, just so long is there a block in our consciousness which prevents our prayers from being answered.

Only in true prayer is it possible to lose all sense of separateness from one another and from one another's interest. Intellectually, it is practically impossible to convince ourselves that another person's interest is our interest, and that our interest is his interest or to believe that we are all equally children of God, because material sense testifies to the opposite. It is only in inner communion with God that we find ourselves in inner communion with man. Then we learn that man does not mean white or black, oriental or occidental, Jew or Gentile: Man means man, that which we are, one infinite equal son of God, but that can never be known through the mind: It can only be known when through communion with God it is revealed to us that we are all one.

Anything that enslaves one enslaves the world; anything that sets one man free tends to free the entire world; anything that impoverishes one man, one race, or one sect impoverishes the world; anything that brings one grain more of supply into the life of an individual, race, or nation tends to set the entire world free from lack. But that, no one can ever accept with his mind, nor could any materialist ever be convinced of its truth. It takes an inner communion with God to reveal why even in the midst of war we should pray for our enemies.

The first thought that comes forth from the materialist when he hears about this radical teaching of praying for our enemies is, "Do you mean that I should pray for my enemy to be successful over me—that he succeed in his deceit, trickery, and conniving?" No, those of spiritual vision would not pray for that at all, but that the enemy's mind be opened and made receptive and responsive to the will of God.

How few people remember that praying for their enemies opens the very doors of heaven, showering its blessings upon them. It matters not whether a nation is an enemy or an ally, the same prayer must prevail, "Open their eyes that they may see with spiritual vision."

Whether the offender be personal, national, or international matters not one whit. There must be the desire that all men be awakened to their true identity and to the Source of all being. Even to those who would crucify him, the Master said, "Father, forgive them; for they know not what they do." To his brethren after they had thrown him into the pit and sold him into slavery, Joseph said, "It was not you that sent me hither, but God." He did not hold them in bondage to their act, but gave them food to carry home, returning good for evil. One of the most important lessons for all of us to learn is that there is no room in the spiritual life for the return of evil for evil—there is no room for anything but a life of forgiveness.

From the moment of waking in the morning until going to sleep at night, there must be periods in the day in which we consciously remember:

*I forgive. If I have aught against any man, woman, or child, here and now I forgive—completely, perfectly, entirely. If anyone's misdeeds persist in coming back to my memory, over and over again I will forgive. I seek no punishment for anyone; I seek no revenge; I seek no justice—I loose everyone and let him go.*

*Father, forgive me my trespasses as I forgive those who trespass against me. Father, open the eyes of the blind. Father, open the eyes of the enemy, whether they are of my household or another's.*

An unfoldment on this very subject came to me the night before I was to give two lectures in a midwestern city. I did not have a single thought or idea in my head about what the subject for the next day's lecture was to be, and although I am quite accustomed to that kind of an experience, it is one which I never particularly enjoy. That night, however, as I was meditating, all of a sudden the word *forgiveness* flashed into my mind.

The first thought that came to me was, "Am I completely purged? Am I entertaining anything in my thought regarding anyone or any group or any nation that might indicate that I have not completely forgiven them?" As I searched within, I could find no one I was holding in bondage.

Then my thought turned the other way, "Am I really forven?" There is not any one of us who has not committed fenses. We may not have considered a particular offense of uch significance in our human life, but in the spiritual life nings that heretofore have seemed of minor importance take on major significance. And so I wondered if I had been completely forgiven and purged of any offenses of which I might have been guilty.

There is a secret about forgiveness: There is not anything or anybody that can forgive us. Therefore, there is not any possibility of our ever being forgiven except under one condition, and that is when there is no possibility of the offense being repeated. In other words, no matter what the offense may have been, as long as there is the potentiality within us of its being repeated, we are not wholly forgiven.

Just let us suppose for a moment that we could carry on a conversation with God about our faults. We confess our fault and we seek forgiveness, and to all this God says, "What? Forgiveness to do it all over again?"

"Oh, no, God, it will never happen again. It couldn't happen again. I've realized the wrongness of it."

At the moment, we actually believe that, but let us not forget that God, being God, sees right through to the center of our heart and knows that the same thing that made us guilty of this act once could make us do it again if similar circumstances arose. And so in His omniscience, God says, "Ah, it's still there. There is still a block within you, and you will continue to be under the penalty of it until you are completely purged of it."

And so we go our way and ponder this response from God. We meditate and look at the situation upside down and from every angle, until all of a sudden we do catch a clear picture not only of the wrongness of what has been done but of the truth that only the state of consciousness that made us commit this offense in the first place could make us do it a second time, and if we find that that state of consciousness does

not exist any more, we have then "died" and have been reborn of the Spirit. Then we can go back again and ask for
forgiveness.

This time, God says, "I don't even know who you are any
more. I don't see anything wrong in you to forgive."

That is the true idea of forgiveness. There really is no God
to forgive. When the state of consciousness that could be
guilty of resentment, anger, jealousy, malice, or whatever it
may have been "dies," there not only is nothing to forgive,
and nobody to forgive, there is not even a remembrance or
a memory—not even a "smell of smoke."

It is pure fiction to believe in some God in heaven who
is going to look down and forgive us while we are out ma-
rauding. True, we can confess our sins and be forgiven in-
stantly, but what about an hour from now when the sin
begins all over again? The Master had a sharp answer for that
—"lest a worse thing come unto thee." He did not preach
a God who permits us to go on our way sinning with im-
punity and then reassures us with a gentle "I forgive you."

Every time we come to a place in our consciousness where
we actually give up our errors of thought and deed, and confess—not necessarily outwardly, but inwardly—to our errors
of omission or commission and feel that deep sense of con-
trition in which we know it cannot happen again, we are
washed white as snow. We are never held in bondage to anything once we have recognized it as error and have forsaken
it. Every time that we come to a place of inner grief over our
errors, we are forgiven. That ends the episode, but it carries
with it the command, "Sin no more, lest a worse thing come
unto thee."

There is really no such thing as one person forgiving another, or God forgiving us: There is only a "dying daily" to
the state of consciousness that accepted good and evil and
acted from that premise, and when that old consciousness
has been purged or is thoroughly "dead" we come to a place
of Self-completeness in God, where we *know*, "I and the
Father are one, and all that the Father has is mine. I am a

child of God, an heir of God, and joint-heir with Christ in God."

Then we can look out on this whole world, and with our new vision behold a world in which there is not a thing anyone has that we want. There is not a sin anyone could commit for which we would hold him in condemnation, criticism, or judgment, knowing full well that the state of consciousness that did it was not really his, but an imposed one, and by imposed I mean a consciousness under the sway of world beliefs and subject to the universal ignorance which characterizes human beings.

When we are fully and completely aware that "I and my Father are one" and when we no longer have any desire for person, place, thing, circumstance, or condition, we are reborn of the Spirit; we are purged because into that state of consciousness we carry with us none of the desires that could result in sin. It did not take a God to forgive us: It took a dying and a rebirthing, and in this new state of consciousness we need no forgiving, because there is no sin.

When we come to the state of consciousness that realizes our Self-completeness in God so that we truthfully can live in the full and complete realization of fulfillment, without a trace of desire or need, there is no block between us and the inner Source of our being, and consequently no block of condemnation, criticism, or judgment, no unfulfilled desire, no greed, lust, or anger. There is only the realization that we are at peace with the Father and with all mankind.

And so as I continued in meditation another question came to my mind, "Have I died to all that is human? If I have, forgiveness is complete; and if I have not, there must be a continual dying until I have realized my Self-completeness in God. I may not be able to praise myself and declare that I am pure, but this much I can do: I can turn and with an open heart forgive every offense that has ever been aimed at me or mine—at me personally, at my family, community, nation, and the world—and entertain a complete and full sense of forgiveness."

With that realization, I settled down into peace and quiet, and a few moments later had to jump out of bed to make a note, and within the next couple of hours I was up four different times, making the notes that became two lectures, lectures that came out of a heart and mind at peace. There was no barrier—no unforgiveness, no sin, no judgment of anyone—nothing but a purity of vision, and in that purity of vision, there was peace.

And so it is that I know now that the subject of forgiveness is an important one in our lives. Over and over again, we must forgive, forgive, forgive, and hold no man in judgment, criticism, or condemnation. A heart that is entertaining any judgment of his fellow man is not a heart at peace. It is futile to seek for peace of mind or soul or peace of anything else until we have fulfilled that Christly message of forgiving seventy times seven all those who offend us, of forgiving our debtors as we would have our debts forgiven.

We store up within ourselves the barriers that prevent the kingdom of God from being established in us by our judgments of people and conditions, and by the desires that still remain in us—not merely the sensual desires but even the desires that are considered good. All of those things operate in our minds to separate us from the realization that that which we are seeking we already are.

In other words, God's grace is not something we are going to attain; God's grace is not something we can earn or deserve; God's grace was planted in us from the beginning, since before Abraham was; and it is only waiting to function in us, but it cannot function while we are entertaining a sense of separation from our good. There never is going to be a chance for us to know harmony until we have completely forgiven and been forgiven, and so purged ourselves that we go to the altar purified.

Some period every single day should be set aside for consciously remembering that we are holding no man in bondage to his sins, that we want no man to suffer or even be punished for them. To forgive means much more than to be content with such cant as, "Oh, yes, I don't want any harm to come to anybody." It is not that simple. It is the ability to sit down and face whatever the enemy may appear to be and realize, "Father, forgive him his offenses and open his eyes that he may see."

No one need be reluctant to forgive the offender his transgressions in the fear that this will set him free to offend again. True, it will set him free, but that freedom will include freedom from the desire to offend. It is not possible for anyone to receive real forgiveness and then to continue in the offense.

*Father, I come to You with clean hands, holding no one in bondage to a duty, nor anyone in bondage as a penalty for his sins. As far as I am concerned, Father, I am willing for You to forgive him. Whatever the sin, it is past, and let it be done and forgotten; and if he does it seventy times over again, forgive him seventy times over.*

*I want no revenge and no vengeance. I seek only to keep myself a pure instrument for Your love and Your grace so as to be worthy in Your sight.*

*I forgive everyone who has ever trespassed against me, consciously or unconsciously, and that forgiveness extends to all those who have trespassed against my religious or political convictions, or my national allegiance. I pray that You, Father, forgive them.*

*Humanly, there are those who owe me debts of duty and of love. I forgive them also. Henceforth, no one owes me anything, not even the obligation of relationship. What they give out of love, I cheerfully receive, but as a matter of duty I expect nothing, and I expect it of no one. I release my friends and my relatives, and everyone: They owe me nothing. It is my privilege and joy to serve them in whatever way You direct.*

*I offer myself an empty instrument: Use me.*

# CHAPTER XVI

# THAT YE MAY BE THE CHILDREN
# OF YOUR FATHER

No part of the Sermon on the Mount is more challenging than its teaching of not only loving our neighbor as ourselves, but our enemies as well. How we react to that command depends upon our answer to the question: Are there two powers? Is there something or someone outside the range of God's power? How great a God do we have? What limitations do we place upon God? To what degree do we believe that God operates on this side of the street but not on the other side?

According to the Master, we are to "call no man [our] father upon the earth: for one is [our] Father which is in heaven." Therefore, no one has an American, British, or Russian father; a white, black, or yellow father; an occidental or oriental father: There is but one Father—the Father in heaven who is the creative and governing principle of each one of us and of all that is.

There may be those who because of their ignorance of this principle do not yet know this truth about themselves and therefore cannot demonstrate it, but that does not prevent our knowing it about them. If we go to the altar to pray, knowing in our hearts that we have not accepted all men as sons of the one Father and therefore brothers, we might as well stop praying for ourselves, get up from the altar, sit down quietly, and decide within ourselves that before we can hope to reach God, we must become reconciled with our brother.

Insofar as we can keep from thinking of a person as a human being—from thinking of his parents, his education, the environment in which he has grown up and now lives, and the accumulation of other factors that may have contributed to his present discord or harmony—and keep our mind stayed on God, realizing that everything that is emanates from God and everybody that is lives and moves and has his being in God, in that degree can we love our neighbor even though he be an enemy.

Let us acknowledge not only that there are sinners, whose offenses are as great as our own, but that there are sinners far worse than we are at this moment, some of whom seem almost beyond human regeneration, much less spiritual redemption. But as far as we are concerned, God is the only Father, the Soul and Spirit of man.

To be spiritually whole, harmonious, and complete, and enjoy the kingdom of God on earth, it is necessary that, in addition to our knowing the truth for ourselves and those within our orbit, we go further afield and know the truth universally so that we do not judge some people as separate and apart from God or as unworthy to be the sons of God, and thereby set up a divided household.

This is not a world made up of separate people and things. Instead, it is like the fingers that rise up from the palm of the hand, which are apparently separate, but nevertheless an integral part of the hand. Whatever takes place in the palm flows up into the fingers. Or it may be likened to the Hawaiian Islands. From the air, they appear to be six or seven islands, each one separate and apart from the other, but if we were able to go down deep enough in the water, we would find that the Hawaiian Islands are really one piece of land—just one island with six or seven upward projections, all one and united in that oneness.

And so it is that if we could see beneath the surface and look into the heart of all mankind, there is no doubt but that we would find that we are all united in the common ground of God. There is one common Ground and that Ground is God. Each one of us is merely a projection, or individualization, of that One, and when we penetrate beneath the surface of the outer life, we soon discover that we are not alone, but that we have a contact with the Source of infinity: We are one with It, and It is flowing out as our individual experience.

If we are honestly seeking God as a way of life and not just as a means to some desired end, not only do we discover that we are one with the Father, but also that there is not a man, woman, or child in the world who is not one with God and who does not also have a spiritual center. It makes no difference what kind of villain or how deep-dyed a devil he may appear to be. In every person, there is a spiritual spark, the common ground of union with God.

It is easy to know this truth about ourselves; it is pleasant and satisfying to think thus about our friends and family; but it is far more important for our own spiritual growth to be able to go beyond seeing only the true identity of those we love and admire and begin to realize that this is also true of those we like least. Regardless of his origin or station in life, God is the creative principle of every man, and all that the Father has and is, is his.

God constitutes individual being, and when we are in the presence of those who understand that, we are at peace, and can live, work, and be joyous in that atmosphere. As we inwardly release everyone from human obligations, holding him only in this united relationship of love, each one feels his freedom, and in that freedom giving becomes a joy because it is not expected or demanded of him or held to be an obligation.

Until a person has had such an experience, he cannot know what love there is between people who have tasted God, nor can he even begin to comprehend how free such a relationship is. On the human level, love of family is for the most part not real love at all, but merely self-love, the desire to possess. Only when the Spirit of God touches one, can he feel spiritual love, and then that love is not limited merely to his own family, but extends to his neighbor and enemy far and near. Human love usually is a completely personal and selfish love, with time, money, and effort for its own, but rarely for others.

When the Spirit of God touches one, however, love of a universal nature springs up which is a love without an object —unless the whole world can be considered its object. Surprisingly enough, this universal love deepens and strengthens the love a person feels for his immediate family; it is a love so complete that each member of the family has a feeling of belonging and yet is separate in the sense that each one is a unit with God. Can human families live that way? Very, very seldom. They live in a constant fear of and for one another, a longing and a desire to see and be in close proximity to one another. That does not exist in spiritual love, and yet in that spiritual love, there is always the joy of tabernacling together.

There is but one principle of life, whether for our own family or others, but knowing that God is the Soul of all being does not mean that God is the parent of mortals. It means that all mortals whether good or bad eventually must "die" to the belief of mortality and awaken to the realization of their true identity. Knowing the truth does not imply a knowing of the truth about human beings or about any condition that is mortal. There is no such truth. Knowing the truth means knowing the truth about God and God's creation, and this knowing of the truth awakens man and lifts him above and out of his mortality.

Everyone has a Soul—not a separate Soul, but the same Soul—and God is that Soul. It is like a tightly closed rose-

168 FROM LAW TO GRACE

bud—so tight and so small as to be imperceptible to a human being. This Soul is not the body: It is consciousness, and the more it can be touched by Truth the more it unfolds as if sunlight were reaching out and opening that bud. Only as we learn to live more and more in the Spirit, do we see and sometimes touch that center which is the Soul of man. We do not see the real person when we look at him as a physical entity: We see only his body.

In order to see anyone correctly, we must develop the habit of looking into his eyes, and then, if we are able to penetrate the depths that lie way, way back of his eyes, we shall see the person in his true identity, behold the reality of his being, and discover that names are but masks for characters in God-consciousness, God-consciousness Itself produced as form. Behind the mask called Bill, James, or Joseph, there is but the one name, G-o-d.

When sufficient wisdom is gained to know that our Soul and the Soul of those we meet are the one and only Soul, a spiritual relationship of harmony, peace, and grace is established, and then the relationships in our lives are not only permanent, but mutually beneficial; whereas, as long as we look to one another humanly, we shall be disappointed. Only in the realization that God is the Soul of man, and that the Soul of man is the source of his good, can freedom from bondage to the material way of life and the material things of life be attained.

Then, every time we go to the butcher or the baker, do business with a broker or a banker, enter our home or church, or go to our business, we shall be seeing the Christ-man, a person without qualities, a person who, we know within ourselves, has the Soul of God, the mind of God, and the Spirit of God.

When someone comes to me for help, I am not aware of his human identity. I recognize, of course, that here is a person, but the only person I see is a person without qualities of his own, a person whose qualities are God-qualities whether or not at the present moment he is bringing them through into manifestation.

In my work in penal institutions, I learned never to look upon the men who were incarcerated in the prison as thieves, murderers, or criminals of varying degrees. To me, they were not prisoners guilty of crimes. They were men, and I did not reach back into their human history any more than I reach back into the human history of the students who come to me. I knew what constituted these men, just as I know, sometimes better than my own students themselves know, what constitutes them, because they are still somewhat immersed in their human identity which they think is composed partly of good, partly of bad, and partly of indifferent qualities. But that is not they at all: That is a person which they have fashioned in their minds, a person molded by certain prenatal experiences, the environment of the early years of home life, childhood, and school days, and then later by personal experiences out in the world. All these influences have formed not a person, but a caricature of the person.

It is much like believing that Laurence Olivier is Hamlet when he has merely identified himself with the character by placing the Dane's costume upon his body, and make-up on his face. With all these embellishments, he is still Laurence Olivier, but if a spectator were very young and attending the theater for the first time, he might believe that this man who was dressed as Hamlet actually was Hamlet, whereas an adult would know that when the final curtain was brought down, all the make-up would come off and Sir Laurence would again be in evidence.

And so with us. We all have human traits—some good, some bad, some indifferent, some we admire in each other, and some we dislike. But that is not you or I. That is the mask that we have built up since birth; that is our presentation of ourselves to the world; that is the part we are playing for one reason or another. But if we could lay that aside, if there were such a thing as a curtain call and we could go to our dressing room and remove all the make-up, we would see ourselves as possessing only the qualities of God with no qualities of our own—no good qualities for which we should expect praise and no evil qualities for which we are to be condemned.

As human beings, we are not spiritual and we are not perfect, despite what we may have been taught in metaphysics. As human beings, we are none of those things: We are people: You are a person, and I am a person, but back of the mask is God, constituting the person that you and I are.

Let us be careful not to endow anyone with qualities of good. No one is spiritual; no one is perfect; no one is good: He is a person—a man, woman, or child, but what he or she really is, is all that God is. So instead of using the words "he," "she," or "you," we go back to the word God and see what it is that God is, and then realize that that is what the person is—God, the invisible, appearing outwardly as God, the visible; God, the Father, and God, the Son—one.

Every person wears a mask hiding his true identity. In fact, *persona* is the Latin word for *mask*; but when we remove that mask of human personality, we discover that whatever God is, the person is. The human personality with its good and bad, beautiful and ugly, rich and poor, up and down, high and low disappears in the realization: "Here is individual being, God expressing Its perfection and harmony." The mere fact that we may be thus looking at a person and the next minute he may steal our wallet does not change the truth of his identity, but merely proves that he has not yet come into the awareness of his true identity.

We owe it not only to ourselves but to the world to know no man after the flesh, but to know every man as we would be known by him, to give up ascribing qualities of good and evil to friend or enemy, to cease thinking about his human history—past, present, or possible future—and to look at him only as a person and see him in his true spiritual identity: "God is the Soul of this individual; God is his mind and intelligence. It is God that is pouring Itself through into expression as individual being." Is there anything in all the world more desired by the human soul than this recognition of his real Self?

At first thought, we might feel that this is being too impersonal, but it is not that at all. It is really being truthful because in practicing this principle, we are beholding people as they really are. When Peter was able to say, "Thou art the Christ, the Son of the living God," it was because he was able to look through the human appearance and see what it was that animated Jesus and made him a savior and a world leader. The outer signs indicated that Jesus was a carpenter, and a rabbi in the Hebrew synagogue, but because of his spiritual discernment, Peter was able to see through that appearance and recognize that it was the Christ that was really functioning as the man Jesus.

If we see the Master in that light, but stop there, we lose our demonstration, because it is not only Jesus who was activated by the Christ: It is you and I as well. In fact, there is not a person in the world of whom it cannot be said, "God, the Father; God, the Son; God, the Holy Ghost."

There is no one who in his spiritual identity is not the child of God, although in the human scene that is far from evident. The human being, living his everyday life, is the man of flesh who is not under God's government and who cannot please God, and that is why he is confused, perplexed, frustrated, diseased, and often poverty-stricken. Not so the children of God: They are not tangled up in the world's troubles—the children of God are free. The children of God are those who have renounced all judgments of good and evil and are convinced in their own minds of the truth about every appearance: "This is neither good nor evil: This is a person. This is neither good nor evil: This is a flower, a painting, a rug. It is not good or evil because God alone is good, and evil is but the hypnotism of this world." When anyone is able to do this, he has made the transition from being the man of earth to being the child of God.

Undoubtedly, there are men and women who are not to our liking, and yet in some moment of transition or conversion their past is wiped out and suddenly they are become new. They look the same; they have the same eyes, ears, nose, and mouth, the same legs and the same body; and often we are not aware that anything unusual has happened to them because the change is an inner change, and it has come about as a transformation of consciousness.

Transformation takes place, not by being transported to some kind of an etheric world or transformed into an etheric body, but by a change of consciousness which recognizes: "I am a person, and since God is the creative principle of my being, all that God is, I am—all that the Father has is mine."

To be transformed from the man of earth to the man of Christ is not a matter of another world: *This* is God's universe; right here and now is the Garden of Eden. There could never be a better place than this very world if so be we can withdraw our judgments—our praise and condemnation—of good and evil. This is the world that every visionary has dreamed of attaining, but nobody can attain the Edenic state while he is hypnotized by the knowledge of good and evil. This can come only as the fruitage of relinquishing not only all judgment or condemnation, but even all praise.

When we are no longer under the hypnotic influence of the pairs of opposites, the world has no power to enslave us. This world is overcome in proportion to our giving up the belief in good and evil, but actually there is no change in the world itself. It appears to be the same: The great difference is that we do not see it the old way any more. For us, there is a different light on it; we now have a different perspective, a different outlook. The people are the same—the same clerks in the stores, the same husband, wife, or child—and yet the whole vision changes the moment we perceive the divine nature of the Soul of man. The transformation has taken place in us.

When we see that nothing but world-hypnotism brings about these varying appearances, we shall no longer fight them, but understand that no hypnotist has ever yet produced anything but a picture or an image, and that this world-mesmerism has never yet created man, woman, or child, has never yet created sin or disease, but only an illusory picture to which the names of man, woman, child, sin, disease, and death have been given.

When we remove world-hypnotism or the belief in two powers from ourselves or any individual, we are free. Then in that day we shall have a new name written on our forehead—a three letter word which can be divided into two words to read, "I Am." That is the truth: I Am—not I was or I will be. I Am at this very moment, and as we realize ourselves as I Am, that I Am-ing becomes a state of continuity, an eternal Is-ing or Am-ing, and the hypnotism disappears.

How can this principle be applied to our human relationships, and more especially how can it be applied to those people who express little of their divine sonship? In order to do that, let us take the person who is the most troublesome in our life, the one we think we would like most of all to be rid of, improve, change, correct, or reform—the one we would gladly exchange for a counterfeit nickel. Now let us see where this person exists. In the first place, how do we know except through our mind that he is the kind of person we judge him to be? Is the person we are seeing an actual person, or does what we have in our mind represent our concept of that person, that is, our opinion or thought about him?

At this moment, if we are quietly reading this book, there probably is no person actually irritating or troubling us; but if we continue to be perturbed about someone, it is because we are entertaining a concept of him, and it is that concept that is causing the conflict within us. If we are disturbed about a person, we may be quite certain that our concept of him is entirely wrong because in his true identity he is God Itself individually expressing on earth, the very Christ of God against whom we are bearing false witness. Therefore, we are the sinner, not *he*, because we are bearing false witness against him by entertaining an incorrect picture of God's own image and likeness, an image so far removed from what the person actually is that if we drew a picture of him as we see him and showed it to him, he would never recognize himself.

Probably the same thing is true of most of the people of this world who know us. If they would write down what they think about us, we would never recognize it as a description of ourselves. If they love us, it is a picture that is far too good and we know it; and if they dislike us, it is a picture that is far too bad, and we know that too. But now we are making exactly the same mistake. The person in whose favor we are prejudiced we think about as being far too good —he does not deserve it humanly; and the other one against whom we are bearing false witness does not deserve that either.

Let us forget the good that we believe about some and the evil that we believe about others and see what the spiritual truth is. This, we can do by taking the one person who seems to be the most objectionable to us. The first thing we discover about him is that we have been mistaken about his parentage because God is his Father. Whatever heritage there is, is of God, and the only qualities any person can inherit are the qualities God bestows upon His image and likeness which include life, love, truth, justice, mercy, integrity, generosity, and benevolence. God's own qualities are His gifts to His children.

God constitutes individual being; and therefore, God's grace is upon this person, God imbues him with His own qualities. He lives and moves and has his being in God's household as a member of the family of God. That is his true individuality and his true being.

This truth about God's creation dissolves whatever human concept we may have been entertaining about any person, because, as we know the truth, the false mental concept which we have built in our thought and which is turning on us and rending us is being dissolved. When next we set eyes upon this troublesome one, love will begin to flow out from us to him because we shall more nearly see him as he is, and when we behold him as he is, we shall be satisfied with his likeness.

The human personality, the human body, the human pocketbook, and the human woes and virtues—all these must be forgotten, and those with spiritual perception must look beyond and above these, realizing: "This is a person, and the reality of his being is God." Such a realization can awaken him to his true identity and dispel the entire illusion of sense which is binding him.

The truth we are knowing is not about a human being but about God, for God is appearing as this individual. Our mind has played tricks on us: We have accepted concepts and believed in them, but now we can see that these concepts are nothing but mental images. The picture in our mind in actuality never was that person: It was a mental concept which we had built, and we disliked the concept that we ourselves had created. When we know that this image in our mind is not truth—is not substance or reality—we can begin to accept God as the creative Principle of life, and we shall understand why we have been told not only to love our neighbor as ourselves, but our enemy as well. In our heart we can say to this person, "I know thee who thou art, the son of God, the Christ. My Father within me has revealed this to me."

# CHAPTER XVII

# YOUR FATHER KNOWETH

There is a way of living, not by might, nor by power, but by the grace of God. However, when we decide what it is we want and how we want it, when we seek to educate God and tell Him how He should operate, we set ourselves up as possessing greater wisdom and intelligence than God, and thereby block the flow of God's grace.

If we understand the nature of God, we will never remind God of anything that concerns us or our affairs, and we shall never be tempted to usurp the prerogatives of the all-knowing Intelligence and Love which "knoweth that [we] have need of all these things."

Is asking God for things an indication that we understand God to be Intelligence and Love, or do not such requests imply that we believe God is witholding something from us? Can we really be concerned about food, clothing, or anything in this world when we have the direct assurance that our heavenly Father knows that we have need of all these things? Did not Jesus instruct us to take no thought for our life, for what we should eat or what we should drink, nor yet for our body, what we should put on?

Why do we seek for bread, wine, or water, for clothing, companionship, money, or capital when the promise is that in His presence there is fullness of life and that it is His good pleasure for us to share His riches. Because of the infinity of God, all that is, is already omnipresent. It is impossible for God to give or send us anything. God does not provide an apple or an automobile. God is the apple; God is the automobile—God appears as.

There is no such thing as God and. It is for that reason that the only demonstration there is for us to make is the demonstration of God's presence. In demonstrating God's presence, we demonstrate life eternal, an infinity of supply, brotherhood, peace, joy, protection, and safety. In His presence there is fullness of life—nothing is absent. When we have God's presence, we have God appearing as good, as clothing, as housing. But there is one requirement: to have His presence—not meaningless affirmations or the mouth ings of the deep truths of Scripture, but His presence.

Where God is, fulfillment is, and through the realization of Omnipresence, all things already exist. God is forever functioning to maintain and sustain the infinite and eternal nature of this universe appearing as. God appears as the daily manna: I am the bread of life—not I will have or should have or will demonstrate it, but I am it; and this I within appears on our table as daily bread. It appears outwardly as transportation or clothing. In the beginning, before time began, God gave Himself to us, and in that giving, infinity was bestowed upon us.

It must be admitted, however, that because of his material sense of existence, man has erroneously accepted the belief that he must go out and earn his living by the sweat of his brow, he must draw it to himself, labor for it, and compete with others. In other words, he is a materialist—a person who wants to get something, who wants to add to himself, achieve, or acquire. On the contrary, the person devoted to the spiritual way of life has little or no interest in accumulating things, whether those things are fame or fortune, because he knows that all that the Father has is already his.

A material world is built upon the unstable foundation of human hopes and fears, but the entire material temple dissolves when we acknowledge that, because the Lord is our shepherd, we need not seek anything, but glory in the truth that God has fulfilled His own being as our individual being on earth. God is Spirit, and when our prayer and our concern are for spiritual realization, we leave the material concept of the world alone and begin to understand that the world of Spirit is a different world, a new world in which God's grace is our sufficiency in all things.

How shall we speak of Grace? It has been called the gift of God, but God has only one gift, the gift to us of Himself. With our human wisdom, we cannot know what God's grace is, and as long as we try to turn and twist it into human language and human meanings, we will never be able to understand God's unadulterated spiritual grace.

God's grace unfolds in ways that we know not of, in unthought-of directions and in forms that we never knew were on earth or, if we did know about them, never dreamed that they would ever become a part of our experience. In each case, God's grace is an individual unfoldment. It will not appear to a person in the form of roses if he does not like roses, nor will it appear to a person as a ticket around the world if he would find greater fulfillment in a little cottage by the sea or up in the mountains. God's grace flows as spiritual activity, but it governs our human affairs in ways that we could not possibly outline or picture.

As we ponder this subject of Grace, there develops within us a sense of independence of the thoughts and things of this world. We begin to feel that if there were not a person in our life to bring anything to us, nevertheless, by morning everything needful would be provided and this through the contemplation of God's grace.

If we attain the consciousness of God, we discover that

there is nothing but God—God appearing as flowers, God appearing as the food on our table, God appearing as the clothing on our backs, God appearing as harmonious relationships, God appearing as the perfect functioning of our minds and bodies. Fighting and battling do not bring this to pass. All that is necessary to bring this into experience is for us to put up the sword, to stand still and see the salvation of the Lord.

There is no higher goal attainable on earth than an inner communication with this Presence that never leaves us nor forsakes us. It does not send us food, clothing, or housing. It *is* food, clothing, and housing. It does not lead us to a fortress or a high tower; it literally *is* the fortress and high tower. There is no sending of anything; there is no giving of anything, except the giving of Itself.

When the realization of the omnipresence of God is attained, there is freedom from worry, fear, lack, and limitation. If a need appears, we retire within and tabernacle with this Presence, and in due time, It will appear outwardly as the very form necessary to our experience.

As we come to this place in consciousness where we are able to relinquish human might and power, human opinion and judgment, a divine Grace, invisible, yet perfectly tangible to the person experiencing it, takes over. We cannot see this transcendental Spirit, hear It, taste It, touch It, or smell It, yet It is here and It is now—we feel It, and we know It. When we let go of our human rights or human will or desires—even the good desires—and absolutely resign ourselves to God's will, It rushes in as if there were a vacuum, and when It takes over, we can feel Its every movement coursing throughout our body, right through the muscles and veins down to the nails. We are one with the rhythm of the universe, and all is well. All that the Father has is now flowing through us out into this world as a divine Grace, bringing to us all that is ours and bringing us to all those to whom we belong.

So we learn that we need take no thought for the things of this world; we need not fight either aggressively or protectively. We can stand still and think no thoughts—just be receptive and let God's thoughts flow to us and permeate our being. And then our work will be accomplished. But I must remind you that Spirit is never working for us. It is working in and through us as we yield and surrender ourselves—even our thoughts—so that God can take over.

Those who have attained even a slight measure of Christhood or spiritual realization are in the world but not of it. They know very little of the sin, disease, tortures, lack, and limitations of human life and are untouched by its tragedies in a personal way. They are aware that these things exist and because of their God-contact they can help others—they can feed the multitudes, heal and comfort them—but they themselves do not require supply or comforting or any of the things the human race finds so necessary. They have surrendered personal might and personal desires and have accepted the love of God, the grace of God, and the government of God as the all and only in their lives.

# CHAPTER XVIII

## YE ARE THE LIGHT

Ye are the light of the world. A city that is set on an hill cannot be hid.

Neither do men light a candle, and put it under a bushel, but on a candlestick; and it giveth light unto all that are in the house.

Let your light so shine before men, that they may see your good works, and glorify your Father which is in heaven.

MATTHEW 5:14–16

We become the light of the world in proportion to our degree of illumination. Some students attain that illumination quickly; and some wait, wait, and wait for the great experience to descend upon them. When it comes, however, it comes suddenly, although the preparation leading up to it may have taken many, many years of studying and meditating, during which time we seem to have made little or no progress. From the first moment, however, that we seriously turned to the attainment of realization, our progress has been rapid even though, to outward appearances, imperceptible.

It is like removing a mountain. From the first shovelful of dirt that is carried away, progress is being made in leveling the entire mountain. But a mountain is made up of countless shovelfuls of earth and stone, and not until many of these have been removed is it apparent that any noticeable progress has been made.

So it is that when we are aware of the density of human selfhood, we know that we are moving a mountain of ignorance, and although a beginning is made with our first serious meditation, progress will not be too evident for a long, long time. Then all of a sudden it seems to burst upon us like a flash of light.

When we have been touched by the Spirit, it is evident in the light shining forth from our eyes and the glow on our face. Outwardly our life changes: Our human relationships change; our nature changes; our health changes; and sometimes even our physical form changes—but only because such changes are the outer manifestation of an inner glory, an inner light, which has been attained by contact with the Father within and which has once again established us in Eden.

Our purpose is to be the transparency through which the Light—not we, but the Light—performs Its mighty works, to be the instrument through which the Divine can manifest and express Itself on earth as It does in heaven. We are never the doer; we are never the actor: We are always the vacuum through which Spirit flows. Let us never for a moment believe that by our spiritual endowments we will ever attain personal or spiritual power. There is no room in spiritual living for egotism or for the exercise of personal power. God does not give His power to another. God does not give His glory to another. The power, the glory, and the dominion always remain in God; and we are but instruments, humble servants or transparencies, through which that Light may shine.

God can find entrance to the world only through consciousness. There was just as much God in the world before the time of Moses, but it had no effect upon the Hebrew people until Moses opened his consciousness, received the

Light, and then was led by God, after which the liberation of the Hebrews was achieved. It was not that there was no God in Egypt—God was there, but there was no consciousness to receive and release God into the world until Moses had his illumination. There had to be a Moses before the Hebrews could be freed.

There was just as much God on earth before the time of Jesus, but it was only when a Jesus appeared and God-consciousness could flow through him that the blessings took place—not only for that time but for all time. Had there been no Jesus in the ship at sea, the storm would not have been stilled. True, in time it would have worn itself out, but it would not have stopped so quickly. It was stilled because of the presence of Jesus Christ. What was it in Jesus Christ that stilled the waves? Were the waves stilled because he had power over them, or because he knew the truth which makes men free and could therefore stand still and let the omnipresence and power of God perform Its function?

There had to be a Jesus before the power of non-resistance could be made evident. There must always be someone through whom the spiritual light can shine and who can stand still and bear witness to the presence and power of God as the only Presence and the only Power. Throughout all ages, the illumination of a Moses, an Isaiah, a Jesus, John, or Paul has resulted in the revelation of harmony to all those able and willing to receive it spiritually.

Looking back and thinking of their developed spiritual consciousness, we would expect perhaps that the influence of these illumined souls would have permeated the whole world and brought harmony and peace to it; yet, as we all know, even while these great lights were walking this earth, the greater part of the world was experiencing untold disasters. That is because no matter how high a degree of spiritual consciousness a person attains, he can bless and help only those who will bring themselves into the orbit of his consciousness. As he becomes a living witness to the Word made flesh, he makes no attempt to exert power: He remains still and beholds the activity of God as It touches the lives of all those around him.

If there is a disaster about us, it will go on and on until it exhausts itself unless one among us knows this truth. If it is to be stopped dead in its tracks, there must be one who can stand still and realize that the grace of God, besides which there is no power, is in operation; there must be one to be completely silent and bear witness to the Spirit which stills the waves.

It is true that a thousand may fall at our left hand and ten thousand at our right. There is not much that we can do about that at this present moment except to prove in our individual experience that because of our conscious oneness with God none of these things can come nigh our dwelling place.

The spiritual word cannot penetrate the human mind; but we can and will help the world rise above war and disease by being the light in our own family, not preaching to them or trying to force them into our way of thinking, but by holding our peace within ourselves and retiring from the battle between good and evil, by going within and realizing that only in the degree that we resist not evil can the peace that passes understanding descend upon us.

If necessary, let us sit in a chair all day and all night, until the Spirit of the Lord is upon us and dwells in us. Then after this principle of *resist not* has been demonstrated in our family, even to some small extent—because it can never be demonstrated beyond their ability to accept it and live up to it—and we know that we are capable of rising above the battle and resting in God, our consciousness of God's presence makes itself felt by bringing some measure of harmony to our community.

To us, it is given to understand how to rise above the battle between good and evil, to know how to still the *storm*, whether at sea or on land, whether a burning fire, an incoming tidal wave, or infection and contagion ravaging the land.

To us, it is given to know how to say, "Thus far, and no farther," and then to stand still, to retire within ourselves from the noise of the battle, without refuting, denying, or fighting, without ever wielding the sword. It is given to us to know that he who lives by the sword shall die by the sword, and therefore we have put up our sword and will never again take out either a physical or a mental sword— not even a spiritual sword. In reality, there is no power for us to oppose physically, mentally, or spiritually, so we need no sword. It has been given to us to know that we live and move and have our being in God in whom is no darkness at all, in whom is no warfare. It is given to us to know that the sovereign, divine remedy for all the ills of the world is to *resist not evil.*

Throughout all ages the world has been blessed with mystics who have made enduring contributions to the spiritual vision of the world, but just as the teaching found in this book cannot be understood by the masses, so the masses have not had the wisdom to heed these mystics or their teachings. No spiritual teaching can ever be understood, believed, or accepted by the unillumined mind which can only grasp what can be seen, heard, tasted, touched, or smelled. The unillumined mind cannot comprehend the spiritual Presence or no-power, because before spiritual wisdom can be understood, the Soul-faculties must be opened, and spiritual discernment aroused or awakened. All human beings are asleep—asleep in the belief of material and mental powers, asleep to the reality of spiritual being, to the transcendental and mystical Presence and Power which men call God.

The scriptures of every faith have revealed that there is a transcendental Presence which, when embraced, encompasses our being and reaches our heart center, setting us apart from the world. Then the germs that lay low the world with grippe and flu do not come nigh our dwelling place, and even if momentarily they do, they are quickly removed. Alcoholism, drug addiction, and juvenile delinquency do not mar the peace and serenity of our household, and if they should touch it, they are quickly dispelled because we have learned how to hide ourselves in the secret place of the most High and live in an atmosphere of love instead of hate, injustice, and inequality.

So it is that every spiritual healing is the result of one individual sitting in the Silence, quietly, peacefully waiting, and then the Spirit comes through the consciousness of that one—the voice thunders in the Silence, and the earth melts.

We become that one in proportion as we learn to be nothing, to be still, and to let that Light act in us and through us and as us. Someday when this world comes to the place of solving its problems by meditation instead of by arms—by the sword—the Spirit will so illumine every situation that there will be no need for the knife or the pistol.

God does not impart His glory to another; therefore, let us not attempt to be spiritually powerful, but be spiritually humble and let God's grace perform Its functions through us and as us. God functions through individual consciousness, and that becomes our consciousness when we have learned to be still enough to hear the thunder of the Silence.

A human being reading or speaking words of truth is not yet the transcendental Consciousness; and yet when that Consciousness has been attained, it is the human being who is the instrument through which it operates. Man born of woman is a mortal, a human being almost completely separated from God and not under God's care or grace. But once this human being has attained the transcendental Consciousness, he becomes that very Christ, and thereafter cannot be separated from It. He is one with It and he is It.

In many orthodox religious teachings, Jesus is set apart as the Christ in the sense of his being Christ-consciousness separate and apart from any other individual as if he of his born humanhood were It. On the other hand, metaphysics tries to separate Christ from Jesus as if they were two. But Jesus is the Christ: The two are inseparable and indivisible one from the other to such an extent that it is almost forgotten that Jesus is Jesus, and he is usually referred to as the Christ.

So is it true of any and every individual who has attained conscious union with God. The only difference is in degree. It takes a person of the attained consciousness of a Jesus to be able to say, "I and my Father are one. . . . Thou seest me, thou seest the Father that sent me." Others do not quite attain that height of realization where they always speak out from the *I*: *I* am the way; *I* am the truth; *I* am the life; *I* am the resurrection; *I* am the bread; *I* am the wine; *I* am the water. That is the transcendental state of consciousness which has gone beyond the human.

In the earliest stages of illumination, there is a sense of twoness. There is a John, Bill, or Mary who is aware of a Presence and a Power—Something overshadowing him, Something helping, guiding, instructing, and governing him. It is within him and functions within and through him, but there is a higher state of consciousness, and that is when there is no person any more. There is just *I* voicing Itself.

That is the Consciousness Itself, and It only comes in the very highest moments of our experience when the Presence is the only being that *I Am*. It was then that Moses transcended humanhood and said, "I AM THAT I AM." It was then that Jesus said, "I am the bread of life. . . . I am life eternal. . . . I am the resurrection."

But even if we do not reach those mountain heights, let us be grateful that we have come to the place where we recognize that within us is Something greater than we are, Something greater than our mentality, experience, or education, Something that can use our mind and body and has knowledge far greater than anything we might have acquired in school or through travel.

This is the goal—the realization that as a person we are a nothingness. We only become something when we are transcended or overshadowed by this Presence within. That consciousness, when it is attained, is the miracle worker. Therefore the only demonstration is attaining it. When we have this Light, there is no miracle then in having health, supply, companionship, or home. Therefore our entire life must be spent in attaining the Light, the transcendental Consciousness.

If the grace of God has touched us to the point where we cannot stop studying and meditating, then we are doing everything that can be done. We cannot hasten the day. We can delay it by ignoring this inner urge to meditate more and to read more, but we cannot hasten it. It comes in its own good time and its own good way.

A human being cannot do this of himself, because to a human being the word of God is foolishness. He has no time for it, no patience with it, and sometimes it can even offend him. But if he is touched with just enough Grace to compel him to keep reading, hearing the Word, or meditating, then he will be led to his ultimate demonstration.

When we are in this Spirit or when It is in us, consciously present, there are not two powers functioning. There is not one power doing something to another power; there is no power of God destroying evil, making evil people good or overcoming lack with abundance.

When this Consciousness is upon us, there are no other powers, and whatever seeming powers there are, are dissolved —not as if these were something being overcome, but as if they were a nothingness fading away.

The world is to be saved by *My Spirit*, but this Spirit operates only through the consciousness of a person who opens himself to It. Therefore, it is our responsibility to become a spiritual rock upon which the harmony of our neighborhood and community, even of our nation, can rest.

We do not need any deep metaphysics: We need to understand the simple little truth that the still small Voice is the power that destroys the illusions of this world. That understanding does not consist of our having a power to do something to error: It consists of the truth that no power is needed to destroy error because error has within itself the elements of self-destruction. We bear witness to that as we stand and look at the unfruitful tree and watch as it withers. We do not wither it: Its own barrenness withers it. So error is dissolved as we sit in quietness and stillness, a witness to the divine Power, and watch as harmony descends upon all around us.

And so step by step we are strengthened until the day comes when we realize that now we can rest at will in God and let that Spirit that flows through us, that Robe that envelops us, be the prayer, the benediction, and the healing to our community and to the world.

We become the light of the world as we bring ourselves to a state of consciousness in which we do not battle the errors of the world, but in which we become completely still and let the Spirit of God nullify and dissolve the pictures of sense. No longer will we struggle with error, but rest, relax, and bear witness to God functioning on earth as in heaven. Above all, we will never forget that we are the twelve, the seventy, the two hundred: We are the light in our community. We are that one, even if there is not another, who will not succumb to the mesmerism of fear, doubt, hate, envy, jealousy, or malice. We are that one who will be a rock in our community, a rock of Silence, welling up within ourselves as peace, and letting that peace descend upon our community.

# CHAPTER XIX

# THE STILL SMALL VOICE

The world has come to a place where it must go beyond power and beyond mind. Is there such a place? Is there a place where physical might and human thought are not power, and where safety, security, and peace are assured?

In a moment of futility and frustration, when every reliance has been forsaken, the answer comes as the voice of God utters Itself, a Voice not in the blustering whirlwinds, nor in the awesome rumblings of the volcano, but a Voice so still that only in the Silence can it be heard, and there It thunders. When we hear that Voice, we need not concern ourselves about protection against bombs; we need not concern ourselves with depressions or recessions. One thing alone then concerns us: the ability to be still and let God manifest and express Himself as the still small Voice within us.

Today, world conditions make our personal problems seem infinitesimal, but whether we are thinking in terms of individual, national, or international problems, basically there is only one problem—material and mental power as against My Spirit.

There is only one enemy—the universal belief that material and mental force can control this world. The enemies confronting us today are not a threatened epidemic of disease, not a devastating condition of weather or climate, not impending economic disaster, nor destructive war: All these are but part and parcel of the belief in material and mental powers.

But are material and mental powers, power, or is the still small Voice the only power? The answer is that there is no power in the visible world, and anything that exists in our mind as an objective thing is not power. Let us never fear an image in our mind whether that image is a person, a disease, or even a bomb. That still small Voice in the midst of us is mightier than all of these, and if we can become so silent that that Voice can utter Itself—even if only as a deep breath or a sense of peace or warmth—this earth will be filled with the voice of God and the belief in two powers will be silenced.

When we struggle and battle with the enemy, whether that enemy is physical and external or mental and internal, we do not win any victories. The real victories are won when we use no power and do not fight our opposition, but rest in the knowledge that all opposition destroys itself.

"The battle is not yours . . . stand ye still, and see the salvation of the Lord." This standing still is not only a refraining from physical and mental power, but from spiritual power as well—a complete relaxing in an ocean of peace. I do not know the process and neither can you, but we can and will witness the fruitage of that stillness and quietness because in the Silence a miracle takes place: The enemy destroys itself and disappears out of our experience—evaporates and dissolves—whether that enemy is a fever, a person, or a nation. We need not fight or struggle with it or with him: We need only be still. We are aligned with a power that is not a power; we are achieving victory without force. We do not even use spiritual force, but our stillness permits spiritual force to use us. Ours is a refraining from power in a Silence which thunders, "I am God; therefore, you be still and rest, for *I* will be with you unto the end of the world. You rest, relax, and be silent."

When we have rested, when we have become still, and when we have permitted the Spirit to permeate mind and body, a Something greater than ourselves goes before us and prepares the way for us: The enmity and opposition dissolve, and we stand within ourselves and marvel, "A mighty work." In a complete Silence, with no attempt to use God, use Truth, or use a power over anybody or for anybody, something takes place within us that dissolves the problems of life and makes the way one of joy and fulfillment.

The only effective and potent weapon against the powers that would destroy the world both physically and mentally is the Silence which comes of the conviction that there is a Something that created this universe and is responsible for maintaining it unto eternity—it is the ability to relax in Silence and let that Something perform Its function.

In that Silence we find Allness. In that quietness and confidence, we find our strength and peace. That is our Sabbath, the complete and perfect universe of the first chapter of Genesis in which we rest from all power, living by the I-say-unto-you way of the Sermon on the Mount. Then we become like "unto a wise man, which built his house upon a rock: And the rain descended, and the floods came, and the winds blew, and beat upon the house; and it fell not: for it was founded upon a rock."

As we meet with problems of every nature—conflicts, enemies, hatred, persecution, injustice—we no longer try to reach out to remove them either physically or mentally, but we rest in His word. We rest from all power, and God works the miracle.

Rumblings of the thunder of the deep Silence of *My* peace reverberate and increase in power until eventually they break every barrier. The mighty noise of the Silence grows in volume until its thunder rends asunder the veils of illusion and God stands revealed in all His majesty, glory, and peace.